A Higher & Deeper Dimension in Prayer

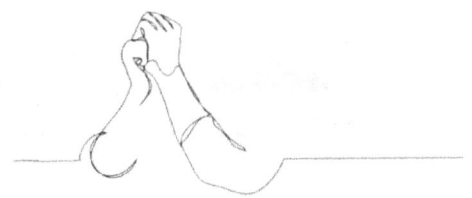

Kirton Whyte
Editor: Danielle Brown-Robertson

A HIGHER & DIMENSION IN PRAYER Copyright © 2022 by Kirton Whyte.

All rights reserved soley by the author. No part of the book may be reproduced, stored in a retreival system or transmitted by any means (mechanical, electronic, photocopy, recording or otherwise) without the written permission of the author.

All scriptures are taken from the Holy Bible Used by permission of Tyndale House Publishers Inc., Carol Stream, IL 30188. All rights reserved.

All definitions are taken from Vine's Expository Dictionary of Old and New Testament Words, copyright © 1997 by Thomas Neilson, Inc. Used by permission of Thomas Neilson Inc., Nashville, Tennessee. All rights reserved.

Book author for conferences, workshops, crusades, conventions, seminars, youth ministry, mentorship, men's ministry, and prophetic and deliverance ministry.

Published by: **Reason with Robdon**

ISBN: 978-1-990266-35-5

Publisher Information

Website: www.reasowithrobdon.com
Follow us: Reason with Robdon
Email: reasonwithrobdon@gmail.com

Table of Contents

ACKNOWLEDGEMENT -------------------------------- iv

INTRODUCTION --5

An Overview of Prayer ---------------------------------------5
    CHAPTER 1 --- 17

NECESSITIES OF PRAYER ------------------------------ 17
    CHAPTER 2 --- 47

Prayers that reach God---------------------------------- 47
    CHAPTER 3 --- 58

Prayer that is Offered in Jesus Name ------------------- 58
    CHAPTER 4 --- 73

Different Ways to Pray----------------------------------- 73
    CHAPTER 5 --- 90

Positioning Ourselves in Prayer ------------------------- 90
    CHAPTER 6 ---104

Prayers for the Manifestation of Miracles-------------- 104
    CHAPTER 7 ---147

ACKNOWLEDGEMENT

Firstly, I want to acknowledge the Lord Jesus Christ, who gave me the grace and strength to complete this book. Secondly, I extend special thanks to my mother, Durzine Robinson Chail (deceased), who was instrumental in motivating me to be the best and reach for the best. She always believed in me, even when I didn't. She knew that I would have reached this milestone one day, but unfortunately, she didn't live to see all this. Thirdly, I want to appreciate my brothers Dalton, Keyan (deceased), and Nerand, my sister Kadian and aunt Audrey for being a source of inspiration and strength during a callous time of my life. Finally, this book would not be such a success without the assistance of the best publishing company, REASON publishing, whose competent team worked assiduously to make the final product of this work possible

INTRODUCTION

An Overview of Prayer

What is a Prayer?

For most persons, when they hear the word prayer, the first thing comes to mind is "Asking" God for something, or "Begging" him to do something.

Prayer is not about merely asking God for something, it is about building a relationship with God, where you get to know him more and more.

God desires constitution more than anything else, that's why he sends his one and only son to die for our sins, so that we can be restored into right standing with him.

Prayer is a two-way communication between us and God, we talk to God and God talks to us.

Prayer is having a dialogue with God. The more we talk to God, the more we get to know him.

If you're in a relationship with someone, how can you get to know that person?

You can only get to know the person by spending quality time with the person. So that quality time would entitle good and consistent communication.

Good communication will lead to better understanding. You cannot understand a person who you have not communicated well with.

The more you understand someone, it is easier to know and to trust that person. You cannot trust someone who you have not known, it is illegal and foolish.

Why is it foolish one might ask?

trust means - firm belief in the reliability, truth, ability, or strength of someone or something.

For a person to have firm belief in someone's ability and strength who you do not know is foolish, what you're simply doing is putting yourself at risk for disappointment and hurt.

Trusting someone is concluding that the person has all the characteristics above.

That is how it is with God; we must communicate with him often enough to know him.

What I am saying is very simple and precise. You cannot pray effectively to someone who you don't know. Because you do not know the person's likes or dislikes, the person's character, will, desire, capability etc.

Some Christians see prayer as an occasional thing, but it is not, it is an obligation. Every believer should pray to God every day, I would say at least twice every day. That's the only way we will grow, in our Faith and devotion to God. Reading the Word and Worship is also important, but my purpose is to stress about prayer.

Why Should We Pray, If One Should Be Asked?

The perfect answer to this question is because Jesus has commanded us to pray. Jesus would not tell us to do something that he has not done.

When Jesus was on earth, he knew the importance of prayer, very often in Jesus's ministry, we saw where he communicated very often to the Father. He would separate himself from his disciples many times to seek the face of his Father.

They are many times recorded in the Gospels where Jesus spent time in prayer.

Let us look at some of the occasions throughout the Gospels where Jesus prayed.

1. *When he was baptized:* - When all the people were being baptized, Jesus was baptized too. And as he was praying, heaven opened, and the Holy Spirit descended on him in bodily form like a dove. And a voice came from heaven: "You are my Son, whom I love; with you I am well pleased Luke 3:21).

2. *Before He chose the twelve Disciples:* - The Scripture states that Jesus went out to a mountainside to pray, and he spent the entire night praying to God prior to choosing his disciples. Can you imagine someone seeking the face of God for the entire night to gain divine insight concerning the decision to make? One of those days Jesus

went out to a mountainside to pray and spent the night praying to God (Luke 6:12).

3. *Just before Peter's Confession in St Luke 9:18-21:* - Once when Jesus was praying in private and his disciples were with him, he asked them, "Who do the crowds say I am?" They replied, "some say John the Baptist; others say Elijah; and still others, that one of the prophets of long ago has come back to life" But what about you?" he asked. "Who do you say I am?" Peter answered, "God's Messiah." Jesus strictly warned them not to tell this to anyone.

4. *At his transfiguration; the revelation of the glory of the Son of God:* - This event occurred approximately six days after Peter's Confession about Jesus. Jesus took with him Peter, James, and John, and led them to the high mountain by themselves. Where he was transfigured before them. His face shone like the sun, and his clothes became as white as light. Just then there appeared before them Moses and Elijah, talking with Jesus. Peter said to Jesus, "Lord, it is good for us to be here. If you wish, I will put up three shelters, one for you, one for Moses, and one for Elijah." While he was still speaking, a bright light cloud enveloped them, and a voice from the cloud said, "This is my Son, whom I love; with him I am well pleased. Listen to him! (Matthew 17:4-6)

5. *When He visited the Lazarus' Tomb:* - Jesus, once more deeply moved, came to the Tomb. It was a cave with a stone laid across the entrance. "Take away the stone," He said. "But, Lord," said Martha, the sister of the dead man, "by this time there is a bad odor, for he has been there four days." Then Jesus said, "Did I not tell you that if you believed, you would see the glory of God?" So, they took away the stone. Then Jesus looked up and said, "Father, I thank you that you have heard me, I knew that you always hear me, but I said this for the benefit of the people standing here, that they may believe that you sent me." (Luke 11:38-42)

6. *For his disciples:* - I pray for them. I am not praying for the world, but for those you have given me, for they are yours (John 17).

7. *For the little children:* -Then the little children were brought to Jesus for him to place his hands on them and pray for them. But the disciples rebuke those who brought them. (Matthew 19:13)

8. *At the last supper:* - While they were eating, Jesus took bread, gave thanks, and broke it, and gave it to his disciples, saying, "Drink from it, all of you. This is my

blood of the new covenant, which is poured out for many for the forgiveness of sin. (Matt 26:26-28)

9. *At the garden Gethsemane:* - He withdrew about a stone's throw beyond them, knelt and prayed, "Father if you are willing, take this cup from me; yet not my will but yours be done." An angel from heaven appears to him and strengthens him. And being in anguish, he prayed more earnestly, and his sweat was like drops of blood falling to the ground. When he rose from prayer and went back to his disciples, he found them asleep, exhausted from sorrow. "Why are you sleeping?" he asked them. "Get up and pray so that you will not fall into temptation." (Luke 22: 41-46)

10. *On the Cross:* - Jesus said, "Father forgives them, for they do not know what they are doing." And they divided up his clothes by casting lots. (Luke 23:34)

"We should also Pray to maintain our relationship with God." The Bible said that the Church metaphorically speaking is the Bride and Christ is the bridegroom.
Let's unpack this phrase:

- *Bride* – is the wife of the groom (woman)
- *Groom* – is the husband of the wife (man)

Based on this context, the Church being the Bride and Christ the groom suggests that thy are in a binding fellowship which would consider to be a marriage.

Marriage is the process by which two people make their relationship public, official, and permanent. It is the joining of two people in a bond that putatively lasts until death, but in practice is increasingly cut short by divorce, separation or even annulment.

It is one thing to get married, and to show the world that you are married. That is opportunity boast about your partner especially when you are having a good time, but certainly another in wanting to break the covenant.

The problem is not getting married, because a lot of people have gotten married and are getting married.

There is a lot of anxiety and anticipation before getting married, people mostly caught up in their feelings and emotions. Only a few people really think about what happens next after marriage.

The biggest challenge is to maintain the marriage. When two people are getting married, they say vows "that they will stay with each other until death, and don't care about the situation." The intention of God from the beginning is that the married vow must not and should not be broken.

How can a married couple stay together?
I heard a lot of people say different things that cause marriages to fail, but I will not get into the ramifications of that now.

But one of the things that causes marriages to fail, is "communication." Lack of communication will damage any relationship; no matter how well you mean it.

Communicate means to share or exchange information, news, or ideas. It means to commune, talk, and interact.

There is no way you can be in a meaningful relationship with someone, and you hardly talk to your partner. It is even worse not talking to your partner at all.

The more you communicate with your partner, the more you get to understand the person. It is difficult to understand someone who you don't communicate with. More, and better communication brings forth a better understanding between spouses.

When there is better, effective understanding in a relationship, then there will be a breakdown of barriers. Why will that be so, because both persons will be more comfortable being open to each other and will speak about any issue freely without holding back. A lot of people kept secrets in their marriages for years, because there is little or no understanding between each other.

When a couple understands each other, it will allow communication to reach another level. The more you are comfortable communicating, the easier it is to know deep things about the person. It is so simple; you can't know a person who you don't have regular and healthy conversation with.

Why am I saying all of this to you? The same in the natural, the same in the Spirit.

We are the Church, the Bride of Christ. Jesus said, that if we abide in him, and he in us, and if we abide in him and his word in us, then we will bear fruit.

We can't stay in a relationship with Jesus if we don't communicate with him daily. The more we spend time talking to God, the more we understand him.

We will understand his person, purpose, personality, and power. Our only way of communication to God is through prayer.

The more we spend time in prayer, The more we will understand Christ. The more we seek his face the more we will get closer to him and know him. The closer we get to God the more amazing we will feel, and the deep things of his kingdom will be revealed to us.

God will not reveal deep things of his kingdom to persons who do not understand and know him.

Psalm 25:14 opines that the Lord confides in those who fear him; he makes his covenant known to them.

Jeremiah 33:3 shares the mind of God – Call to me and I will answer you and tell you great and unsearchable things you do not know.

When you know God:

- You live in every way to please him because you fear him (reverent, adore, and respect).

    Deuteronomy 10:12 (NIV) – And now Israel, what does the Lord your God ask of you but to fear the Lord your God, to walk in his ways, to love him, to serve the Lord your God with all your heart and with all your soul, and to observe the Lord's commands and decrees that I am giving you today for your own good.

1Peter 1:15-16 (NIV) – But just as he who called you is holy, so be holy in all you do; for it is written: Be holy because I am holy.

- You will know his will – the will of God is revealed to us when we know him, and by constant prayer, we will be able to know the will of God for our lives.

Christians who know the will of God for their lives, pray differently from those who don't because they know exactly what God wants them to do, where he wants them to go, and what is expected of them.

This book is designed to teach you in depth, and to reveal the deep thing of God about prayer. It will give us a clearer and better understanding of prayer and will prepare and position us as believers to be more effective in prayer.

CHAPTER 1

NECESSITIES OF PRAYER

Important things to do before getting into prayer

Acknowledge God

We live in a time when most Christians are unaware of how to go to the throne of grace. Casually, some approach prayer to God with little or no value. Being privy to this, I believe Christians need to be taught how to pray; they need to know the fundamentals and to whom they are praying.

I have listened to how many people pray, especially Christians, and their initiation involves asking God to do this or that as if they are trying to persuade Him to do what they desire. Some will go to the extremes of binding and losing, tearing down, etc., without even taking the time to acknowledge the presence of God.

How would you feel if someone came to you everyday begging, without acknowledging who you are to them or even saying thanks for what you have and continue to do for them? Wouldn't you appreciate people who have a heart of gratitude towards you?

Which set of people would you prefer to give things to freely?

The grateful. Persons who genuinely love and appreciate all you have done for them.

The ungrateful. People present when it is convenient for them. They may not love you for you but for what they can gain.

The Bible said that God is a Spirit, and they that worship Him must worship Him in Spirit and truth. This same God manifests himself into three distinct personalities: God the Father, God the Son, and God the Holy Spirit. As evident in the Bible, the triune Godhead has separate roles, but unites in mind, will, character, power, and authority.

In the Old Covenant, God the Father manifested himself among His people as He spoke to them and made his power and purpose known.

In the New Covenant, God the Son was manifest before humanity. He took the form of man and related to us in human form. He had feelings, emotions, and a mind. "He suffered pain and agony and died for us. While Jesus was on earth, shortly before he ascended to heaven, he told his disciples that he would send the comforter who would remind them of everything he taught them. He is God the Holy Spirit. It is of utmost importance to note that the Holy Spirit is a person. He is the one who reveals Jesus to the Kingdom of God to us and resides inside our bodies, His temple" (1Corinthians 6:19).

Understanding the role of the Godhead is crucial because of their presence and involvement when we pray. "The Holy Spirit helps us in prayer when we don't know what to pray for; the Spirit himself intercedes for us with groans that words cannot express." (Romans 8:26)

As we pray, it is by the name of Jesus that God the Father answers our prayers. As we come to understand God, we must acknowledge Him. But what does that signify? To acknowledge means accepting, admitting, or recognizing something or the truth or existence of something in its English definition. In Greek, it is epiginosko, which means to know thoroughly or to identify a thing to be what it really is.
Let us dissect the definition a little more.

Accepting someone or something implies taking or receiving willingly or agreeing to, especially with consent, favor, or approval. When you accept God for who He truly is, you embrace His presence and His goodness. Without a doubt, you will know that he is who he said he is in scripture because you have identified Him and are connected to him through a personal and divine encounter.

You accept that he is:

- Our Creator
    - 1 Peter 4:19

- Eternal God
    - Deuteronomy 33:27

- Jehovah-Sabaoth ("The Lord of Hosts.")
    - Isaiah 6:1-3

- El-Elyon ("The Most High God")
    - Genesis 14:17-20, Isaiah 14:13-14

- El-Roi ("The strong one who sees"
    - Genesis 16:13

- El-Olam ("The everlasting God")
    - Isaiah 40:28-31, Deuteronomy 33:27

- El-Shaddai "The God of the mountains or God Almighty"
  - Genesis 17:1; Psalm 91:1

- Abba Father
  - Romans 8:13

- El-Elyon
  - Genesis 14:17-20

- Elohim (The Only Living God)
  - Genesis 1:1, Psalm 19:1

- Adonai (Lord, Master)
  - Malachi 1:6

- EL-Kanna (The Lord is "Jealous."
  - Gen 14:18,22

- Jehovah Yahweh
  - Genesis 2:4

- Jehovah Maccaddesheh ("The Lord they sanctifier"
  - Exodus 31:13

- Jehovah-Rohi ("The Lord my shepherd")

- Psalm 23:1

- Jehovah Shammah ("The Lord who is present")
  - Exodus 15:2

- Jehovah-Rapha "The Lord, our healer."
  - Exodus 15:26

- Jehovah-Tsidkenu ("The Lord is our righteousness.")
  - Jeremiah 23:6

- Jehovah-Jireh "The Lord will provide"
  - Genesis 22:13-14

- Jehovah-Nissi ("The Lord is our banner"
  - Exodus 17:15

- Jehovah-Shalom ("The Lord is peace")
  - Judges 6:24

- Jehovah-Geo ("Redeemer")
  - Exodus 8:10

- Jehovah-Hamalech ("The King")
  - Psalm 24:8

- Jehovah-Hashopet ("The Judge")

- o   Isaiah 49:26; 60:16

- Jehovah-Hoshe'ah ("The Lord Who saves")
    - o   Psalm 98:6

- Jehovah-Gibbor ("The Lord is strong and mighty.")
    - o   Judges 11:27

- Jehovah-Kabodhi ("My Glory")
    - o   Psalm 24:8

- Jehovah-Machsi ("My Refuge")
    - o   Psalm 3:3

- Jehovah-Magen ("MY FORTRESS")
    - o   Psalm 91:9

- Jehovah-Bara ("Creator")
    - o   Joshua 3:13

- Jehovah-Chereb ("Glorious Sword.")
    - o   Isaiah 40:8

- Jehovah-Eli ("My God")
    - o   Deuteronomy 33:29

- Ancient of Days

- Daniel 7:9

- God Almighty
  - Genesis 17:1
  -
- Counselor
  - Isaiah 9:6

- Great Shepherd
  - Hebrews 13:20

- Great High Priest
  - Hebrews 4:14

- Deliverer
  - Romans 11:26

- Consuming fire
  - Deuteronomy 4:24

- God Who Sees Me
  - Genesis 16:13

- Everlasting Father
  - Isaiah 9:6

- Bright Morning Star

- Revelation 22:16

- Beginning
    - Revelation 21:6
- End
    - Revelation 21:6
    -
- Author of our Faith
    - Hebrews 12:6

- Author of Life
    - Acts 3:15

- Arm of the Lord
    - Isaiah 53:1

- Anointed One
    - Psalm 2:2

- Alpha
    - Revelation 22:13

- Advocate
    - 1John 2:1
- Amen
    - Revelation 3:14

When we acknowledge God, we admit the aforementioned about God and more. To admit means, we confess that everything written about God in the Bible is true. We don't need to be hesitant in our beliefs because of the revelation we receive.

When something once hidden is revealed to you, nothing or no one can tell you otherwise. The more we admit who God is, the more we allow him into our lives, homes, place of worship, etc. We demonstrate to God that we are indeed grateful for all he has done. We also prove our love for Him and express our appreciation of His person and mighty works.

Let us look at some of the ways we acknowledge God:

1. In Praise and Adoration

Praise denotes the expression of approval or admiration for someone or something (to commend, applaud, eulogize, compliment, hail). While to adore means deeply love and respect (someone) (to cherish, treasure, prize, reverence, exalt, extol, magnify, worship).

I firmly believe that today's church (believers of Christ, the assembly, the called out one's, those living and following Christ Jesus) lacks an understanding of what it means to praise our eternal God. They may be aware of its theoretical sense but not the practicality of the same. Intellectual knowledge from biblical studies regarding praise is ineffective without practice.

Since my conversion at age 19, I have seen the repeated cycle in church services where the pastor, praise and worship leader, moderator, or any other person leading asks the congregation to praise God. They would casually shout praise the Lord or hallelujah instead of taking time to acknowledge God's sovereignty and faithfulness. People are getting saved by the thousands each day, and the Kingdom of God is growing. But how many of these believers will know what praising God entails to practice it effectively. It is not about making noise and crying, though the same may be involved. Praising God is about expressing oneself to God with kind words about Him freely as we commend Him for all the things, he has done for us.

How many things has God done for us, individually and collectively as a people? It is countless. Typically, when someone has done something special or significant, our first impression is to commend them for their achievements. We recognize them for their hard work and accomplishments, especially when they made many sacrifices. There is also the tendency to hail celebrities, whichever capacity they are in, whether in sports, music, etc.

Let us take, for example, Usain Bolt; whenever he completes a race, supporters from all over the world would go crazy, creating an eruption in the stadium. Bolt is loved not only for his contribution to sports, though he transformed track and field, but also for his personality as he loves to entertain.

What is my point in using Bolt as an example? The sad reality is that while the world knows how to praise persons for their achievements, the Church of the living God is clueless about how to honor their God and Lord. If we who say we love God and believe in Jesus would see the importance of praising Him for what he has done, what he is doing, and what he will do, we are guaranteed a deeper experience with Him.

We can agree with the songwriter, "when I think of the goodness of Jesus and all that he has done for me, my soul cries out hallelujah! Thank God for saving me."

Were you born saved? Certainly not! We are saved by grace through faith. It is the blood of Jesus that bought our redemption. If it had not been for the sacrifice of Jesus, when he died on the cross for our sins, we would not have access to God the Father. He carried our burdens, sorrows, shame, and diseases and nailed them to the cross. That's enough to give God praise. How many of us were bound, trapped, defeated, and dead in sin, but the blood of Jesus rescued us from the trap, curse, and bondage of Satan? Like John Newton, we can sing, "Amazing grace, how sweet that sound, that saved a wretch like me, I was lost, but now I'm found, was blind, but now I see."

Our true praise draws God's attention and pulls His presence to us; hence, the more we praise Him, the closer he is to us. The Bible declares, "God inhabits the praises of his people." God lives within our praise; it creates an atmosphere for God to dwell whenever we praise Him. Notice the difference when people praise God sincerely; there has always been a manifestation of his glory.

Remember now that we are in an intimate relationship with the Lord. He has feelings and emotions, and how we treat him will determine the outcome of our prayers for our lives. How we treat God will determine what God does for us on our behalf. Show appreciation for Him, and He will react to your cries and rescue you.

It is one thing to praise God but another to adore him. To adore, one must show love and respect due to a deep and shared intimate relationship. Our relationship with God is judged by the way we treat him. It is impossible to treat God with little to no respect and honor when we genuinely know and love him because the essence of the word adore is to love "deeply." This is not a frail love that the world talks about when they say I love you yet treat the individual as an outcast or infidel.

We, therefore, are required to do whatever it takes to make God happy and comfortable in the relationship to offer our most sincere adoration.

Then, we will come to cherish Him more than gold, diamond, or Pearl. Have you ever had something that means a lot to you, whether you received it from someone or purchased it yourself? One of the first tendencies is to take a good look at that thing until one's eyes are comfortable in that moment. You may later find the best and safest place to put it after satisfying yourself and check it frequently. This is because it is very precious to you, and you desire to make sure that you take good care of it.

If we as people can cherish vanity to that extent, what about God, who is more precious than material things? In fact, He is the one who blesses us with the blessings. But sadly, material things receive better treatment and more attention from us than God.

It is evident, only those close to God will adore him and have the desire, urge, passion, and determination to adore him. In this context, to know God does not merely involve those baptized, speaking in tongues, attending every service in the church, being active in a particular ministry, or even working for the Lord because you can but lack a relationship with Him. Knowing signifies having a personal and divine encounter with the Lord, being transformed into his image, and manifesting the fruit of the Spirit. The Holy Spirit must be the one governing your life, and as a result, you develop a deep and intimate bond with Jesus where you can't get enough of him in your life.

We can praise and adore God in songs, such as, for example:

- This is my desire, to honor you, Lord with all my heart I worship you.

- Falling in love with Jesus, is the best thing I ever done.

- You are awesome in this place, Mighty God.

But most importantly, we must also praise and adore Him in the way we live. Our character should reflect our sincere love for God. As believers, we are letters to this world and will be read daily. We therefore have a responsibility to provide the most authentic representation of God and our commitment to Him. How we live can seriously impact people's lives, whether negative or positive. That's why Jesus said, "You are the salt of the earth. But if the salt loses its saltiness, how can it be made salty again? It is no longer good for anything except to be thrown out and trampled by men."

"You are the light of the world. A city on a hill cannot be hidden. Neither do people light a lamp and put it under a bowl. Instead, they put it on a stand, and it gives light to everyone in the house.

In the same way, let your light shine before men, that they may see your good deeds and praise your Father in heaven".
(Matthew 5:13-16 NIV)

2. *With our attitude*
Attitude is a settled way of thinking or feeling about someone or something, typically reflected in a person's behavior.

When we acknowledge God with our attitude, we become fully convinced of who God is and our transformation through His word. Our attitude changes, which alters the way we think and act. We yield ourselves to God's power, dominion, and authority in an attitude of surrender.

God loves when His people come to Him with the attitude and heart of surrender. This proves that we are totally dependent on Him for His help and guidance.

Our attitude towards God will determine our acknowledgment of Him. He requires a heart of humility and brokenness because that's when we are our strongest. Then, His strength is made perfect in our weakness, and His grace is poured out in our lives to carry us through our situations. This is what God told the Apostle Paul during one of his most vulnerable times by a situation he was unable to overcome. Maintaining humility is like having a sweet fragrance for God to smell. God hates pride, which fosters man's selfish views, desires, passion, will, and mind.

Approach God with your brokenness, and He will draw nigh to you and intervene according to your cry. Be completely humble and gentle; be patient, bearing with one another in love (Ephesians 4:2)

Humility will change the way you live and treat others. Do nothing out of selfish ambition or vain conceit. Rather, in humility, value others above yourselves. (Phil 2;3)

It is God's way and will prove that you fear and love Him. "Wisdom instruction is to fear the Lord, and humility comes before honor." (Proverbs 15;33)

Humility is the fear of the Lord; its wages are riches and honor of life (Proverbs 22:4)

Before God blesses or elevates us in His Kingdom, our attitude must be one of humility. "Humble yourself therefore, under the mighty hand of God that he may lift you up in due time." (1 Peter5:6)

"Humble yourselves before the Lord, and he will lift you up." (James 4:10)

Pride will remove God's presence from your life faster than anything else. The scripture says that God opposes the proud but gives grace to the humble. Pridefulness invites the devil to take advantage of us, creating ruin in our lives. Pride brings a person low, but the lowly in spirit gain honor. (Proverbs 29:23)

When pride comes, then comes disgrace, but with humility comes wisdom. (Proverbs 11:2)

God's ears are always open to hearing the cry of the humble and the broken so that He can intervene on our behalf. "If my people who are called by name, shall humble themselves, and pray, and seek my face, and turn from their wicked ways; then will I hear from heaven, and will forgive their sin, and heal their land." 2 Chronicles 7:14

3. *Confession And Repentance*
Genuine and sincere confession is what God requires and will accept. I firmly believe that many believers are ignorant of the importance of confession and repentance regarding our relationship with God and the differences between the two.

If our prayers are to be effective, we will have to practice daily confession and repentance. Confession is a formal statement admitting that one is guilty of a crime or offense. However, repentance is to feel or express sincere regret or remorse about one's wrongdoing or sin. It entails turning from sin and dedicating oneself to the amendment of their life. Repentance is more than simply acknowledging wrongdoings; it is a change of mind and heart. It involves turning away from sin and turning to God for forgiveness.

Psalm 51 is an excellent example of confession and repentance. The Psalm of king David was made after he committed adultery with Bathsheba, and God sent the Prophet Nathan to confront him. After the confrontation, David was sorrowful in his heart, realizing the magnitude of the act he had committed. He then started crying out to God for mercy as he expressed how much he was sorry and needed help.

David realized the divide created between him and God, placing his life in jeopardy, both spiritually and physically. The only solution to get back in line with God to follow His pre-steps is confession and repentance.

Whenever we hurt someone, especially one we love, we first seek to apologize for the ill done because of its potential to close the relationship door between them and us. This is because the individual would have trusted us in their heart, sometimes even secrets, only to be betrayed.

Confession will ease the tension between the two parties, softening the heart of the hurting party and eventually restoring the broken relationship.

Have you ever been in a situation where you were hurt by someone you loved and was close with? As time goes by, the hurt and pain inside no doubt increases, causing possible resentment in your heart, especially when you know you didn't do anything to deserve the damage done. If the person humbled themselves and confessed to you, though it may go through a process, your heart softens towards them because of the potency of confession.

The Bible expresses that "a man who covers up his sins cannot prosper, but if we confess our sins to God, He is faithful and just to forgive us our sins, and to cleanse us from all unrighteousness" 1 John 1:9. The avenue of our hearts and life must be clean to connect to God and have His divine intervention.

Whenever we wrong God, we need to come to the consciousness that God has feelings and will be hurt by the same, but once we acknowledge it and go before Him broken and sorrowful, He will pardon us.

Hebrews 4:15-16 said, for we have not a high priest which cannot be touched with the feeling of our infirmities; but is in all points tempted like as we are, yet without sin. Let us come boldly unto the throne of grace, that we may obtain mercy, and grace to help in time of need.

The major problem is not so much that we sin against God, though it is entirely wrong, it is when we refuse to come back to God and tell him sorry for the same and are determined to refrain from repeating the act. God is always merciful, loving, kind, slow to anger, and always abounding in love; He will never turn his people away from His presence whenever they seek forgiveness. "If we confess our sins, he is faithful and just to forgive us our sins, and to cleanse us from all unrighteousness." 1 John 1:9

Confession is vital for our prayers to be answered because it puts us back in right standing with God. God does not delight in answering prayers when our vessels are dirty.

In Isaiah chapter 1, Isaiah condemned the people for their hypocrisy (insincerity and double standard lifestyle) because they had exhibited evil behavior and injustice while continuing to bring offerings and sacrifices to God. They pretended to worship God, but time was about to reveal their evil deeds. We see how worship, praise, and prayer become a disgrace to God when our hearts are not truly devoted to him and his holy, pure, and perfect ways.

"And when you spread forth your hands (in prayer, imploring help), I will hide My eyes from you; even though you make many prayers, i will not hear. Your hands are full of blood!

Wash yourselves, make yourselves clean; put away the evil of your doings from before My eyes! Cease to do evil, learn to do right! Seek justice, relieve the oppressed, and correct the oppressor. Defend the fatherless, plead for the widow. Come now, and let us reason together, says the Lord. Though your sins are like scarlet, they shall be as white as snow; though they are red like crimson, they shall be like wool." (Isaiah 1:15 -18)

Before God can hear and accept our prayers, our hearts will have to be clean before God. We must rid our hearts of unforgiveness, hatred, bitterness, etc.

"If I regard iniquity in my heart, the Lord will not hear me Unforgiveness is one of the biggest hindrances to our prayers without us even knowing it, and the longer we take to get rid of it, the more our connection from God fades." (Psalm 66:18)

4. *Entertaining God* (Third necessity)
Entertainment entails providing someone with amusement or enjoyment. Have you ever been attracted to someone and tried everything possible to cross their path and gain their attention when they are around? We ought to make the same deliberate effort to earn God's attention.

There are many ways in which we can entertain God:

1. *Singing:* - a beautiful voice can shift a person's focus with its magnetic energy, no matter how tight their schedule may be—listening to singers like Whitney Houston, Celine Dion, Brian McKnight, etc., gives chills. Singing is a powerful tool we can use to draw close to God, the creator. Using melodies, tell Him how sweet and

awesome He is, how special He is to us, and that there is no one like Him nor can be compared to Him.

2. *Dancing* – Did you know that you can dance and entertain God? Ask King David. David danced before the Lord with all his might, arrayed with fine linen. (2 Samuel 6:14) When you value the presence of God, you will do whatever it takes to keep it. David was so overwhelmed to see the Ark of Covenant return (The presence of God), that he forgot his status and identity as the King; he was not concerned with anything else at that moment in time. He was entertaining God's presence with his praises. "Praise his name with dancing, accompanied by tambourine and harp." (Psalm 149:3). Before David danced before the Lord, he heard that the Lord had blessed Obed Edom and his household because of the Ark of God. He then brought the Ark of the Lord from the house of Obededom into the city of David with gladness. David recognized the power, goodness, and benefits of the presence of God and the importance of entertaining God to see His wonders. Whenever we dance before God in the anointing, His presence will show up in our lives and bring results.

3. *Clapping of hands* – Scriptures speak about the clapping of hands and its importance to the Lord. Clapping our

hands is a great way to entertain God, as He is moved by sound. There are three reasons why people clap hands unto God:

- Because of something that God has done in the past for them. It could be an expression of gratitude to God because He healed, delivered, or provided for them.

- For things that God is doing for them presently. The awe of God's manifestations in our lives and its effect may propel us to clap our hands to the Lord. Most people who are beneficiaries of God's goodness and grace will feel the urge or push to clap their hands, entertaining His continued presence.

- The final reason why people clap their hands to the Lord in entertaining Him is because of something that they anticipate Him doing in their lives. Clapping our hands and making music pulls God's presence to us. Whenever we draw God's attention, He has the power to do wonders in our midst. *"For thus says the Lord God; Because thou hast clapped thine hands, and stamped with the feet, and rejoiced in heart with all they despite against the land of Israel." (Ezekiel 26:6)*

"Men shall clap their hands at him and shall hiss him out of his place." (Job 27:23)

4. *Stamping of feet* - Let's reflect on the era of the Old Testament. God would wage war against the enemy, and in my reflection, I imagine the people of God stamping their feet as if they were crushing the head of their enemies as they marched, giving praises to God. They knew the importance of relying on God's intervention and would consult with Him for direction as they offered worship to Him.

An excellent and powerful example of stamping, as it pertains to entertaining the presence of God, is seen in the book of Joshua, chapter six (6). The Bible said that the Jericho wall was very tall and wide, and the children of Israel had to pass over it to enter the city. Joshua commanded the people to march around the wall for six days, and on the seventh day, they should march around the wall seven times. Can you imagine the feet of those fighting men on the ground pounding it as if they wanted to sink it? The beauty of the story is that it was God's instruction, and in obedience, they marched, shouted, and the walls came down. It wasn't the stamping or shouting that caused the wall to come down, but it was the presence and power of God. Their stamping entertained the presence of God and did wonders for them. *"For thus says the Lord God, because you have clapped your hands and stamped your feet and rejoiced*

with all the scorn of your soul against the land of Israel."
(Ezekiel 25:6)

"Turning towards the woman, He said to Simon, "Do you see this woman? I entered your house; you gave Me no water for My feet, but she wet My feet with her tears and wiped them with her hair." (Luke 7:44)

Prayers that Invoke the Supernatural and Overrule Darkness:

"In the beginning, God created the heavens and the earth. And the earth was without form and void, and darkness was upon the face of the deep. And the Spirit of God moved upon the face of the waters. And God said, let there be light: and there was light." (Genesis 1:1-3)

As it is written, "I am in Christ, and Christ is in me", John 14:20, and because I belong to God, I am His, John 17:9. I command things that are needed in my life this season, this day, this time, this hour, to appear now, in the Mighty Name of Jesus.

- I command all the resources needed to fulfill destiny, to appear and fall in their rightful places in Jesus' powerful name.

- I command money to come forth, and it is connected to me like steel attached to a magnet in Jesus' name. By the word of God through the power of the Holy Ghost, In the Mighty Name of Jesus, I call forth everything that is needed in my life for it to be a success. I call them from the north, south, east, and west.

- For every darkness in my life, I command the light of Christ to destroy it.

- For every financial struggle in my life, let there be light.
- Let there be peace in my life, family, ministry, and marriage in the Name of Jesus.

- Let everything that opposes the light of Christ catch fire.

- Let every demonic power sent to destroy purpose be paralyzed and burnt. Every demonic gadget dies by fire, in Jesus' name.

- I declare that the light of God will destroy all darkness and expose all the works of hell.

- Put your hand on your chest and repeat, "I was born to win, I cannot be defeated, I will never go under, I am more than a conqueror through Christ Jesus."

- Now place your hand on your head and say, "may every darkness in my mind be burned by the Holy Ghost fire and leave."

- May every ungodly and evil thought burn by fire! I will have the mind of Christ.

- Lay hand on your belly and declare, "every darkness in my body, be exposed by the light of Christ. Every ungodliness in my body is burned by fire, and every demonic stronghold is paralyzed by fire.

- I vomit out every demonic substance in Jesus' Mighty Name.

- I puke out everything that is not of God that has lodged in my body. Begin to vomit now.

- My body is the temple of the Holy Spirit therefore, no demonic spirit can live within me.

CHAPTER 2

Prayers that reach God

Prayer of Faith

We should have sincere faith that God will answer, and act based on our requests whenever we pray. We should believe that God will supply whatever we ask of him, knowing that He has the power and ability to do the same.

If we pray with doubt, it defeats the purpose of our prayer from the onset. Doubt and faith are incompatible because of their inability to produce the same result. Faith requires total confidence in God, who is committed to standing by His word. We can rest assured that He will give us what we desire because of His integrity. Faith is of God. All believers were given a measure of faith when they accepted Jesus as their personal Savior.

Doubt, on the contrary, is ungodly, and the devil is the culprit responsible for putting it in the minds of God's people. His intention is for us to abandon our purpose and destiny in Christ. Doubt embodies uncertainties about God's ability to bring things to the past in our lives. It is like saying God is not good enough, strong enough, effective enough, or capable enough to provide whatever we ask of Him.

Doubt is a killer. It drove Eve to disobey God and cost humanity everything. She allowed the serpent to convince her to eat off the tree in the middle of the garden, which God told her and Adam not to eat off. The serpent persuaded Eve, insisting that God's instruction was flawed. In other words, he implied that God is a liar who had tricked them because He did not want their eyes to be opened as His (God). The devil's indication that it was ok for her to pick and eat the fruit, for she would be like God was absorbed, doubt entered her mind, and everything began to head into destruction. She felt that God was not a promise-keeping God and whatever he said was not valid. That's what doubt will do; it will cause you to see God in a different light other than He authentically is.

Doubt will shift your concept of who God is. The implications are tremendous because how you perceive Him will determine how you look at him, trust him, treat him, and impact how much you expect from Him. If you see God as the covenant-keeping God, you will live and honor your covenant relationship with him, knowing that whatever agreements you share will not be broken on his part. If you see God as the promise-keeping God, you will hold him accountable for every promise He gives because of the assurance that it will come to pass, no matter how long it takes. If you see God as the all-powerful God, you will be confident that nothing is hard or impossible for him to do.

Frankly, doubt is a sin and is the absence of faith. Hebrews 11:6 declares, "But without Faith, it is impossible to please him: for he that cometh to him must believe that he is and that he is a reward of them that diligently seek him." Believers who refuse to hold God at his words cannot please him and will not obey him. The more we have faith in God, the more expectations we have of him.

Expectations create a strong desire and patience for what God has in store for us. Any presence of doubt devalues, disregards, and undermines God's power, ability, and authority. Praying in faith is asking God for things that align with his word and will with confidence.
"But let him ask in faith, nothing wavering. For he that wavered is like a wave of the sea driven with the wind and tossed." James 1:6

We serve a supernatural God; nothing is complex or challenging for him. What seems impossible with man is possible with God because He takes pleasure in doing supernatural things in our lives. God delights in healing, granting breakthrough, deliverance, restoration, etc., to His heirs. Whenever we ask anything of God, we must do so with expectations, knowing that our Father, God, will not disappoint us or put us to shame.

We have every reason to believe in God whenever we pray.

1. *Our past experiences with God in prayer.*

If many believers testified more boldly about God's goodness and greatness through his miraculous manifestation of miracles in our lives due to prayer, we would shake the world. Numerous miracles are locked up in our testimonies, and once released, they will free those waiting for their breakthrough. Others need to hear about the marvelous work of God because of prayer. If doubt starts to creep in when you pray, reflect upon all God has done for you and use it as strength to believe Him for what is to come.

"Jesus said unto him, If thou canst believe, all things are possible to him that believe." (Mark 9:23)

"Jesus answered and said unto them, Verily I say unto you, if ye have faith, and doubt not, he shall not only do this which is done to the fig tree, but also if he shall say unto this mountain, Be thou removed, and be thou cast into the sea; it shall be done. And all things, whatsoever ye shall ask in prayer, believing, he shall receive." (Matthew 21:21)

Let me share one of my testimonies. I made a drastic move in 2007 when the Lord instructed me to start Bible College. I was working in a position for a few months, and reality came crashing upon realizing I would have to leave, unaware of how to start or finish. There was no money to cover the deposit on my tuition; I was only sure of money to purchase shoes, uniforms, and writing books.

I can recall walking into Bible College well suited in my uniform without a dime; all I had was faith and the promises of God through direct prophecy that He was going to pay my school fee and that I must not worry about anything. Whenever I was summoned to the office about my school fee, I would inform the secretary that the payment would soon be credited to my account, even though I did not know where to get the funds. After these meetings, I would return to my secret place, cry out to God, and remind him of his promises to not put me to shame but pay my school fee in full. After praying, I always found peace because a call from the office secretary would notify me not to worry. After all, someone paid the balance in full. This occurred during my three-year tenure at Bible College. I obeyed and trusted in the Lord that his promises would come to pass. Every time that I was called to the office for school fees, I would go back to the Lord and cry to remind him of his promise and believed that it would come to past, and every time the money would appear, if you asked me where it came from, I couldn't tell, all I can remember was that somebody paid it.

It didn't stop there; I graduated from Bible College on a Saturday and was scheduled to start my studies at Caribbean School of Theology (C.S.T) the following Monday to pursue my Bachelor's in Bible and Theology. I was uncertain about going because I didn't have the funds, but I ordered the books for the course on credit by faith. I felt the pull to go, so I went into class on Monday. I recall walking in with no money for boarding accommodations, food, or the course. As I trusted God, I became content and found peace until the person in charge of registration requested that all the money be paid. I quickly informed her that she would get the money by the weekend because I trusted God. The weekend came, and there was no money to fulfill the promise; I thought long and hard about the situation but embraced myself and prayed again for God to give me a miracle. By the following Wednesday, the money was paid in full. This happened for two and a half years, but I always ordered my books and believed that God would provide the money to complete the course, and He never disappointed me. I completed Bible College and Caribbean School of Theology without owing any money.

2. *We should believe when we pray because of other people's experiences.*

I am sure that you have heard countless testimonies of how God came through for his people due to prayer. The Bible is filled with testimonies and experiences of God's mighty acts, whether through deliverance, protection, transformation, healing, or provision.

Let us look at two of them:

Abram and Sarai, Zechariah, and Elizabeth – Both Sarai and Elizabeth could not have a child; they were barren. And note, both women were married to Godly male leaders chosen by God.

Abraham was the first Prophet recorded in the Bible and became the father of many nations. He was a man of faith and is mentioned throughout the Bible because of this remarkable character trait. Zechariah was a priest who served as the mediator between God and his people. He took the sacrifices of the people and offered them to God. He was also a man of faith and prayer who walked before the Lord, holy and blameless.

Even though both men were devoted to God, great leaders, and had a strong faith in Him, they also had wives who could not have children. However, God promised them that he would open their wives' wombs. Because of how things unfolded in their lives, both men doubted God when faith mattered most. Zechariah was dumb from when the angel Gabriel appeared to him until his child John the Baptist was born. Abraham listened to Sarai's foolish advice and went and had sexual intercourse with Hagar, his maidservant, who ended up costing him much pain.

It doesn't matter who you are, the title you possess, the ministry God called you to, or even the great and mighty things that God used you to do; you can still doubt God at the most crucial time before the manifestation of his promise. In the end, Sarai gave birth to Isaac, and Elizabeth gave both to John the Baptist. We know about the great things that both did, especially John the Baptist, who was the forerunner before our Lord Jesus preaching the Kingdom of God to the people and forgiveness of sins.

"Therefore, I say unto you, what things ever desire, when he prays, believe that he receives them, and he shall have them." (Mark 11:24)

Prophetic prayers

Father, may you enforce your will over my life this day, in the Mighty Name of Jesus Christ. As it is written, God will never leave us nor forsake us. With the Power and Authority invested in me, I bind the works of Satan for my life, in Jesus' Mighty Name I pray.

God, we thank you, that you have given us the power to bind and to loose, and with that power, we bind the devices of Hell in the Name of Jesus Christ of Nazareth.

- I bind every satanic harassment.

- I bind every satanic provocation.
-
- I bind every satanic projection.

- I bind every demonic interference in the Mighty Name of Jesus Christ, and I release the judgment of God against them now.

- I bind every demonic limitation.

- I bind every demonic illusion.

- I bind every demonic conjunction.

- I bind every demonic interception in Jesus Mighty Name I pray.

Lay your right hand on your belly and repeat this prayer:

- Every poisonous substance that I have consumed whether, by drinking or eating, I command my body to reject them now, in the Mighty Name of Jesus Christ.

- May I vomit them up now in Jesus' Mighty Name I pray (begin to vomit).

Lay your hand on your head:

- I command every demonic spirit that has been sent to influence my mind, may they catch fire now in the Mighty Name of Jesus.

- I command their powers to lose their hold of my mind in Jesus' Name.

- I have the mind of Christ; hence no demon will mess up my mind.

- I declare that I am a child of the King, and nothing that the enemy establishes will be able to steal my inheritance, in the Mighty Name of Jesus Christ.

- I declare that I am the head and not the tail.

- I declare that I am above and not beneath.

- I declare that nothing will be able to separate me from the Love of God which is in Christ Jesus

- I declare that I am persuaded that, even life or death, or principalities or powers, things present or things to come nor angels, will be able to pull us away from Christ Jesus. As it is written, we are the righteousness of God in Christ Jesus.

CHAPTER 3

Prayer that is Offered in Jesus Name

When we pray, we should pray in Jesus Name

When we do something in someone's name, we do it with the person's permission, approval, and authority.

- True followers of Christ are given the permission, approval, and authority to use the Name of Jesus when praying.

- Praying in Jesus' name doesn't mean that we must use His name at the end of every word, line, or prayer for God to hear us.

Have you ever heard people pray, and after every other word they say, in the Name of Jesus? The same is not required once we become one with Christ through His blood and are totally dedicated to Him, walking in obedience to His commands. As believers, we have been crucified with Christ and have His permission, approval, and authority to pray in His name. When we possess that authority, we have the confidence and assurance that Christ Jesus will hear and answer our prayers.

St John 14:13-14 declares, "and whatsoever he shall ask in my name, that will I do, that the Father may glorify in the Son. If he asks anything in my name, I will do it."

We will always get results whenever we pray in the Name of Jesus. Those who have had encounters with Christ will comprehend the power in His Name; not a clichéd statement because you can repeat it.

The Name of Jesus has mighty power to accomplish anything we desire. Heaven shakes, opens, and reacts, whenever we mention the Name of Jesus.

I heard a story about a mother who went out with her child. While walking on the road, the child ran out of her hand and tried to cross the street, but a trailer swiftly approached the child to crush him. The helpless mother could not do anything in her power to help her baby and cried out JESUS! JESUS! As she cried out, the trailer stopped immediately. The driver came out and stood before the trailer, trembling like crazy. Overjoyed, the mother ran toward him and thanked him for saving her child's life. The confused driver told the mother to calm down because she didn't know what had happened. He explained that he did not stop the trailer; at the speed at which the trailer was coming, there was no way he could have stopped it. The mother then remembered that it was when she cried out to Jesus that the trailer stopped.

Praying with the approval and authority of Jesus can change any given situation. His name has mighty power and brings deliverance, healing, peace, transformation, happiness, restoration, provision, and guidance.

Prayer that is Offered According to God's Perfect Will
This is the most crucial part when it comes on to prayer. Many people know how to pray; some have a lot of words, while others generally put their words together to flow smoothly. One must be aware that it is one thing to pray, but another to pray according to the will of God. Our prayers cannot be effective if we pray outside the will of God because He will not grant us our desires only, but whatever is in accordance with his perfect will.

As people of God, we sometimes ask God for things based on our desires, emotions, circumstances, and feelings. However, we must recognize that God doesn't bless us based on our feelings. He blesses us based on what is in His plans.

Therefore, crying daily to God and asking him for things that are not in line with His will, cannot shift or move Him to act because he knows what is best for us.

Often, our prayers have been ignored and neglected by God because the things we have asked for were not in God's plan for our lives. But how can we know what is in the will of God to make our request? We can only know the will of God through His word. The more we read, study, and meditate upon God's word, the more we will understand His will. God will always stand by His word, so we can confidently believe what He says in His word.

God doesn't want his people to be ignorant; In His word, we are charged to "to study to shew yourself approved unto God, a workman that needeth not to be ashamed, rightly dividing the word of truth." (2Timothy 2:15)

Studying the word will cause us to live and pray effectively. God desires for us to pray intelligently, according to His purpose and desires. God has many gifts for us, but there are also things He doesn't want us to have, so we must know the difference. If we are unaware of God's plans, we will miss them. Why? Because we will not know what to ask him for.

1 John 5:14 declares, "and this is the confidence that we have in him, that if we ask anything according to his will, he heareth us."

"God wills for us to be prosperous and be in good health even as our souls prosper." (3 John 1:2)

"God wants his people to be prosperous, not to beg or borrow, or to live in poverty. He wants us to live happily and serve him well and to be content in this life." (Jeremiah 29:11)

It is in God's plans and purpose to give us peace. Peace with Him, peace with ourselves, and peace with others. God doesn't desire for us to live in confusion because then, the state of our minds will not be focused or stable, and e need a clear and sound mind to be more effective in our lives. The mind is often classified as a battlefield. It's where battles start and are won. May your mind be free and focused on Christ.

Many are challenged because of the misconception that we aren't to desire wealth as believers. We must change this perspective because it is in the plan and purpose of God for his people to have wealth. I have seen believers afraid to own businesses, houses, and riches. If you should speak about riches in Christ among some believers, they look at you strangely, but it ought not to be so. "And you shall remember the Lord your God, for it is He who gives you the power to get wealth, that He may establish His covenant which He swore to your fathers, as it is this day." (Deuteronomy 8:18)

I recall an experience I had when a lady came to me and said, Pastor, I want you to help me pray about something. I asked her about what, and she told me that she was in love with someone, and the person was in a relationship but wanted to come out because his partner wasn't treating him well. She asked me to help her pray to get the man for herself. Imagine this woman is married and has not yet divorced her husband. After questioning her, I understood that the man she wanted me to help her pray for was her church sister's husband, with whom she was good friends. They prayed together, sang in the same choir, and were in the same group. There is no way I would have helped someone like that to pray. That was madness, and there is no way the Lord would have answered such a request. They both were married, and God honors marriages. Inherently, her motive was wrong; the whole thing was a mess.

I have also encountered people who prayed for people to die to get their assets or partners. What am I saying here? Sometimes we make ridiculous demands to God, so God ignores the request when we pray.

"And he said unto them, when he prays, say, Our Father which art in Heaven, Hallowed be thy name. Their kingdom came. They will be done, as in Heaven, so on earth." (Luke 11:2)

Persistent Prayer
We must continue to P.U.S.H - pray until something happens

We must continue to knock on Heaven's door until God

gives us an answer
God's word tells us to "ask," and it shall be given, "seek," and we may find, "knock," and the door will be open unto us. (Matthew 7:7)

To ask is conveying something to obtain an answer or some information or requesting that someone does something. On the contrary, to seek is an attempt to find something (search for, try to find, look for, be on the lookout for, be after, hunt for). Knocking implies striking a surface noisily to attract attention, especially when waiting to be let through a door.

Persistent prayer does not necessarily mean asking God for the same thing repeatedly. God already knew what we needed before we even asked him, and it is His desire and will, to bless us and make sure that we are well taken care of. We are fully aware that God is our Shepherd; however, He expects us, His children, to exercise our faith when we pray.

Therefore, persistently praying is essentially praying with expectations. Through our faith in Christ, we progressively eliminate doubts from our minds, so whenever we feel that God is not coming through for us, we won't become impatient with God because of the flesh, it is natural for a believer to get worried when praying to God for a particular situation, and it seems as if God is not listening or is taking too long to come to our rescue. Having such a door open will allow doubt will creep in, and the enemy will tell us all sorts of lies for us to give up and lose faith in God. Instead of worrying, we must remind God of His word and encourage us to wait on Him. It is not always a good feeling to wait on the Lord, but it is always the best thing to do.

"Wait on the Lord be of good courage, and he shall strengthen thine heart: wait, I say, on the Lord." Psalm 27:14

"Wait on the Lord, and keep his way, and he shall exalt there to inherit the land: when the wicked are cut off, thou shalt see it." Psalm 37:34

Even when you feel you're going out of breath and can hardly pray, persistent prayer pulls you together to push yourself still. "I am weary of my crying: my throat is dried: mine eyes fail while I wait for my God." Psalm 69:3

"But they that wait upon the Lord shall renew their strength. They shall mount up with wings as eagles; they shall run, and not be weary; and they shall walk and not faint." Isaiah 40:31

Since my conversion, there have been several times where I have had to be consistent in prayer. Some stubborn situations in my life caused me to persevere in prayer before experiencing my breakthrough. I recall my experience when

I was to migrate to the United States. Upon my visit to the embassy, they took my passport for almost a month because they made every effort to deny me entry. They called several people, including two of my senior Pastors, inquiring about me. When I realized what the enemy was trying, I went into prayer and fasting for about seven days, three of which were part of my easter fast. During those days, I went without food for three days and nights, praying and seeking the face of God for a breakthrough concerning my visa. On the final day of the fast, I saw a vision where I was driving, and police stopped me and conducted a thorough vehicle search, but could not find anything illegal, so I was allowed to go free. Upon waking up, I knew God was showing me immigration could not find any fault with me for withholding the visa. The same morning, I received an email that I should come to pick up my document. As believers, we ought not to be discouraged when we pray once, and nothing happens. I charge you to keep praying and pressing until something happens.

"Pray without ceasing." 1Thessalonians 5:17

We must always pray, in and out of season. The more we pray, the stronger we become and the more power we will receive. Only persistent prayer can unlock Heaven for our sake.

Pray in the Spirit

We primarily pray with the Holy Spirit's help to pray in the Spirit. The Holy Spirit as we know Him is the third person in the Godhead; He is "Omnipresent" because He can be found everywhere, "Omnipotent," being all-powerful, and "Omniscient," because He is all-knowing.

Therefore, the Holy Spirit is everywhere. He sees everything going on in our lives; the good, the bad, and the indifferent, and He is aware of our pain, concerns, etc. There is nothing unknown to God about us. He knows when we live down to when we get up, so even the request we make in prayer cannot be hidden from Him, even before we make our approach. Psalm 139 proclaims, "and guess what, he has the power and the authority to guide us in our prayers, and to direct our prayers for it to be answered by God."

You may ask about this correlation to praying in the Spirit; well, this understanding is imperative to pray effectively.

We must also know that praying in the Spirit is dying to self and yielding to the control of the Holy Spirit. He is the one who guides us into the right way to pray. "In the same way the Spirit helps us in our weakness. We do not know what we ought to pray for, but the Spirit himself intercedes for us with groans that words cannot express." (Romans 8:26)

When we allow the Holy Spirit to guide our prayer, we will not pray amiss. He is the best teacher, and no matter the mastery of pedagogy, no one is as reliable as He is. In this wise, the scripture declares, "but as it is written, the Eye hath not seen, nor ear heard, neither entered the hearts of man, the things which God hath prepared for them that love him. (1 Corinthians 2:9)

Our prayers will always be off the surface, on point, and direct because the Holy Spirit knows all things. God will grant us everything we need and pray about or for according to His perfect will.

If you have the eyes of the Spirit, you can tell whenever the Holy Spirit is praying through someone.

1. The person will be out of their usual self. The Holy Spirit will take total control of the individual during prayer so that the voice of God may be heard, touching everything God expects.

2. Self has no place whenever the Holy is praying through someone. During this time, the presence of God overrules and over-shadows the individual in prayer. The experience is supernatural as even the very appearance and voice of the praying person changes because of the indwelling presence of God.

Prayer in the Spirit is vital in the body of Christ. Conclusion: there are so many things happening simultaneously, so we must be very alert and vigilant in prayer, totally dependent on the Holy Spirit to help us in prayer. Unless the Spirit of God leads us, our prayers will not be direct and effective.

Prayers Against Hindrances

- I declare that I will live a holy and pure life before God in Jesus' name.

- I declare that I will walk in fellowship with God and will worship Him in Spirit and truth according to John 4:23
  "But the hour is coming, and now is, when the true worshipers will worship the Father in spirit and truth, for such the Father seeks to worship him."

- As the word declares in Psalm 66:18, "If I had cherished sin in my heart, the Lord would not have listened." If I have any unforgiveness in my heart, I repent. Everyone I have held in my heart; I release them now in the mighty name of Jesus.

- I declare that bitterness will not be a part of my body, and I command every anger in my heart to come out now with the blood of Jesus.

- I confess my sin to God because I know that He is faithful and just to forgive me of all my sins and unrighteousness according to 1 John 1:9.

- I put a stop to all ungodly communication from my mouth and corrupt talk, and I declare that I will use my mouth to speak godly things so that I may not grieve the Holy Spirit (Ephesians 4:30)

- My body will not hold grudge or malice in Jesus' name, and every filthy thing in my body must come out now from the root in the mighty name of Jesus Christ of Nazareth.

- I declare that my life will be a life of prayer so that there will be no room for evil and ungodliness.

- Even when I don't feel like praying, I commit to praying because I know that prayer will keep me rooted and grounded in Christ.

- I declare and decree that I will always pray in the Holy Ghost because that's the only way my prayers will be effective.
- (Jude 20)

- I will allow the Spirit of God to lead me in every prayer session because only He knows the heart and mind of God.

According to Proverbs 28:9, the word of God is very important for our prayers to be answered. I declare that I will not neglect the word of God but will spend quality time studying and living according to the principles so that there can be no blockages to my prayers in Jesus' Name. As it is written in Psalm 119:9, the only way a person can cleanse his ways is by taking heed to the word of God. I declare that the word of God will take root in my heart and arrest me to bring total change and deliverance in my life in the mighty name of Jesus.

CHAPTER 4

Different Ways to Pray

1. We can use the scriptures to pray, using direct or indirect words or phrases.

Here are some direct scriptures some use in prayer:

Psalm 23 – The Lord *is* my shepherd; I shall not want. He makes me to lie down in green pastures; He leads me beside the still waters. He restores my soul; He leads me in the paths of righteousness for His name's sake. Yea, though I walk through the valley of the shadow of death, I will fear no evil for You *are* with me; Your rod and Your staff, they comfort me. You prepare a table before me in the presence of my enemies; You anoint my head with oil; My cup runs over. Surely goodness and mercy shall follow me all the days of my life, and I will dwell in the house of the Lord forever.

Psalm 91:1-11 – He that dwelleth in the secret place of the most High shall abide under the shadow of the Almighty. I will say of the Lord, he is my refuge and fortress: my God; in him will I trust. Surely, he shall deliver me from the snare of the fowler and from the noisome pestilence. He shall cover them with his feathers, and under his wings shalt thou trust: his truth shall be their shield and butler. Thou shall not be afraid for the terror by night; nor for the arrow that flieth by day; Nor for the pestilence that walketh in darkness; nor for the destruction that wasteth at noonday. A thousand shall fall at thy side and ten thousand at thy right hand, but it shall not come nigh. Only with thine eyes will thou behold and see the reward of the wicked. Because thou hast made the Lord, which is my refuge, even the most High, they habitation; There shall be no evil befall thee, neither shall any plague nigh thy dwelling. For he shall give his angels charge over there in all thy ways.

Psalm 27:1-5 - The Lord is my light and my salvation; whom shall, I fear? The Lord is the strength of my life; of whom shall I be afraid? When the wicked, even mine enemies and my foes, come upon me to eat up my flesh, they will stumble and fall. Though a host should encamp against me, my heart shall not fear; though war should rise against me, in this will I be confident. One thing have I decided of the Lord, and that I will seek after; that I may dwell in the house of the Lord all the days of my life, to behold the beauty of the Lord, and to enquire in his tempo. For in the days of trouble, he shall hide me in His pavilion; in the secret of his tabernacle shall he hide me; he shall set me upon a rock.

Psalm 24 - The earth is the Lord's, and the fullness thereof; the world and they that dwell therein. For he hath found it upon the cease and established upon the floods. Who shall ascend into the hills of the Lord? Or who shall stand in his holy place? He that hath clean hands, and pure heart, who hath not lifted his soul unto vanity, nor sworn deceitfully. He shall receive the blessings from the God of his salvation. This is the generation of them that seek him, that seek their face, O Jacob, lift your heads, O ye gates; and be ye lifted up, ye everlasting doors; and the King of glory shall come in. Who is the King of glory? The Lord is strong and mighty, the Lord mighty in battle. Lift your heads, O ye gates; even lift them up, ye everlasting doors, and the King of glory shall come in.

2. *We can pray Silently (1Samuel 1:13)*

Silent prayer is just as effective as any other prayer. In this type of prayer, we speak with God in a still small or low tone from our hearts. In 1 Samuel 1:13, we see Hannah praying this prayer when she was barren and her mistress Peninnah was provoking her regularly because she had children, and Hannah had none, though they shared the same husband. In desperation, Hannah reached her breaking point, cried out to the Lord, and went without food. The bible mentioned that Hannah was praying with her lips moving, but none could hear her voice because she prayed inwardly from her heart.

Many people believe the misconception that if a praying person does not make a lot of noise, their prayers will not be effective. However, God is not moved by noise or our emotions. The only thing that will move God is a broken and sincere heart. David said, "a broken and contrite heart God will not despise" (Psalm 51:17).

God is more concerned about the heart of an individual than anything else. Those who believe that only amplified praying yields a response from God are in error. God's desire is for His followers to be intelligent, not arrogant, and ignorant. The scripture declares, "my people perish (destroyed) because of lack of knowledge" (Hosea 4:6). Knowledge in this context is understanding "The Word of God," which is loaded with accurate information according to which we should live. The word of God is vital because it sustains, guides, heals, delivers, prospers, and restores people.

Incorrect information will lead people in the wrong direction and cause some to make a lot of errors, eventually leading to destruction. The church needs the correct teaching to operate in the way God has commanded us to walk, talk, and live like Jesus. On this premise, we see the importance for preachers and teachers of the word to spend quality time reading, studying, and meditating on God's word and spending quality time in His presence to impart accurate and correct information to His people.

The way many believers think has to do with the teachings that they receive from others. For this cause, some will criticize each other about how they pray. Every mode by which people pray is effective once their heart is right with God. One can attest that we do not always pray the same way because situations differ and will determine our approach to prayer. Therefore, each mode of prayer warrants equal respect; a person's spirituality cannot be subject to the way they pray but their relationship with Jesus.

It is good to pray silently at times because of the magnitude of life's experiences that occasionally dwindles one's vitality to pray aloud. Today, many Hannahs in the church face tough times, not knowing what to do, where to turn, or why things happen. Here, whispering or inwardly expressing the words of one's feelings becomes ideal.

I have had situations where I could not pray out to the Lord but whispered or beseeched in my heart. In 2018 my mom passed away from her battle with cancer and went home to be with the Lord. She was everything to me, my motivator, inspiration, and hero. When she passed, my world had stopped, and my mind was displaced. I could hardly pray because of the pain inside, knowing that my mom was gone. The only thing I found the strength to do was commune with God silently.

Two weeks after I buried my mother, I got a text message from my uncle that my father had passed. Yes, I lost both parents less than two months apart, which was tough for me to focus. Imagine the hurt, but our faithful Father understood my tears and gave comfort despite it all.

3. *We can pray aloud (Nehemiah 9:4, Ezekiel 11:13)*

As the words suggest, this is when a person lifts their voices to the Lord in prayer. It can be during the time of corporate prayer and even individual prayer.

There are several examples of people praying loudly before God:

- In Acts 4, when Peter and John were arrested and flagged because they were preaching that Jesus had resurrected from the dead and healed an incapacitated man to make matters worse.

The leaders and high priests gathered and questioned Peter and John, asking; by what power, or name, have ye done this? "Peter filled with the Holy Spirit, said unto them, Ye rulers of the people, and elders of Israel, if we this day be examined of the good deed done to the impotent man, by what means he is made whole; be it known unto you all, and to the people of Israel, that by the name of Jesus Christ of Nazareth, whom he crucified, whom God raise from the dead, even by him doth this man stand here before you all." Acts 4:8-13

Peter even went on further to challenge them that salvation is found in no other name but Jesus, and that only in the name of Jesus can people be saved. (Acts 4:7-12)

When they were released, Peter and John went back to the believers and told them all that the Priest and leaders had done and spoke. In response, the believers lifted their voices to God with one accord and said, "Lord, thou art God, which have made heaven and the earth, and sea, and am, that in them, who by the mouth of your servant David has said, why did the heathen rage, and the people imagine vain things? The Kings of the earth stood up, and the rulers were gathered against the Lord, and against Christ. For a truth against thy holy Child Jesus, whom thou hast anointed, both Herod and Pontius Pilate, which the Gentiles, and the people of Israel, were gathered, to do whatsoever they had, and their counsel determined beforehand to be done. And now Lord, behold their threats: and grant unto thy servant, that with all boldness they may speak thy word, by stretching forth thine hand to heal; and that signs and wonders may be done by the name of thy holy child Jesus. And when they had prayed, the place was shaken where they were assembled; and they were all filled with the Holy Ghost, and they spoke the word of God with boldness."

People often pray loudly when there is a serious, desperate situation and the need for God's divine intervention with urgency. They have a saying, "desperate time calls for desperate measures." The idiom points to the pursuit to do whatever it takes to have a matter resolved on occasions where a challenging situation requires an immediate solution.

As a minister of the gospel for 14 years, I've had my fair share of trials, tribulations, pains, disappointment, failures, and agony. During these moments, I pray louder, especially when the warfare gets intense, and I cannot ease up in prayer. The bible declares that we fight against principalities, powers, rulers of darkness, and spiritual wickedness in high places. The demons sent by the devil to attack our lives are not ordinary; they have one assignment to destroy our purpose and destiny and will do the extreme for our souls to be lost. These spirits will work and operate through any available avenue, system, or person. They work through the Government, media, and various industries (food, clothes, music, etc.). Whenever these demonic elements attack us, we cannot pray any usual or friendly prayers; our prayers typically are aggressive.

There are times when I have been pressed on every side, and I know it is because of the devil. The moment I recognize his plans, I begin to bind and loose, taking authority over the system and devices of satan over my life's purpose, health, ministry, and family. The enemy doesn't want to see the people of God prosperous; thus, he will thrive to bring confusion, discomfort, discontent, and disruption to our lives. Once you recognize his plans, start praying aloud with authority.

There are times when principalities and I come face to face, and I must stand up under the power of the Holy Spirit and fight back in prayer, with my voice sounding the trumpet. I can recall many junctures when the enemy sent legions of demons to destroy me, and the Holy Spirit had to arise in me with power and might so I could stand up in prayer. As I pray aloud, I usually feel as though I have the strength of ten lions and could just rip the devil apart. I firmly believe that I penetrate the forces of darkness more, cause chains and shackles to be broken faster, burdens to be lifted easier, and see yokes destroyed more with this strategy.

In Acts 16, Paul and Silas were beaten and thrown into prison after casting a demon out of a slave girl the leaders used to make a lot of money through divination. We are told that while Paul and Silas were there in the dark cell with soldiers surrounding them, instead of cursing God and complaining, they did something that a lot of Christians wouldn't do. Remember now that Paul was a Roman citizen, and they did nothing wrong to be thrown into prison, but they maintained their purity in the adverse situation; they prayed. "At midnight, Paul and Silas prayed and sang praises unto God: and the prisoners heard them. And suddenly there was a great earthquake so that the foundations of the building were shaken: and immediately all the doors were opened, and every one's bands were loose." (Acts 16:16-26)

4. *We can pray through Groaning (Not using human words)*
"Likewise, the Spirit also helpeth our infirmities: for we know not what we should pray for as we ought: but the Spirit itself maketh intercession for us with groanings which cannot be uttered." *(Romans 8:26)*

This verse expresses that the Holy Spirit intercedes from within us. As the helper, He helps us, takes hold of our weaknesses, and pleads the case on our behalf before God as our intercessor.

During this time of prayer, we are helpless in finding the right words to pray. Being vulnerable and powerless to keep ourselves in the realm of prayer, the Holy Spirit communicates with the father through our desperate inner cries and the longing of our hearts.

Groans are characterized by a low creaking or moaning sound when pressure or weight is applied. Praying with groaning is when a believer comes to God in prayer and cannot adequately express their needs and desires in words because of the pain felt on the inside. This pain can be in two ways:

a) It could be the believer's problem that has become such a heavy burden for them to carry and even express to God because of its effects. One must always be mindful that even though we are serving God, we are not immune to challenges. Therefore, we will be faced with challenges each day, and sometimes the situations may become unbearable. Let us go back to Hannah's position in 1 Samuel 1. This is also a perfect example of groaning from a personal perspective. The bible conveyed that because Peninnah continued to provoke Hannah, she became bitter of soul, prayed unto the Lord, and wept sore. Hannah continued praying before the Lord that Eli marked her mouth. Because she prayed in her heart with only her lips quivering, he thought she had been drunk and said to her, how long will you continue to be drunk? Then charged her to put away the wine he assumed she was drinking. We must be careful not to misjudge when persons pray with groaning; less, like Eli, we impose wrongly due to our lack of understanding of the person's situation.

b) The second way a person groans in prayer is when the people of God are in severe crisis. Throughout the lives of the prophets, we see how they often cried to God on behalf of the people whenever they sinned against God. An example of this is in 1 Samuel 7:8. "And the children of Israel said to Samuel, cease not to cry to the Lord our

God for us, that he will save us out of the hand of the Philistines." This prayer is a cry for mercy.

5. We can offer prayers to the Lord through Singing (Colossians 3:16, Ephesians 5:19-20)

"Speaking to yourselves in psalms and hymns and spiritual songs, singing and making melody in your heart to the Lord; Giving thanks always for all things unto God and the Father in the name of our Lord Jesus Christ." Ephesians 5:19-20 (KJV)

In the early church, hymns played a significant role in expressing the believers' faith in God and the message of Christ being songs of praise that focus on His character and personality. By singing hymns, we honor God with our praise and worship, spontaneous words from our hearts with great joy and peace to invoke the presence of the Holy Spirit while pouring out ourselves to God.

All Christian music genres in the church or private should be primarily directed to God as a prayer of praise or sincere request. We can find a perfect example of prayer to the Lord through singing in 1 Samuel 2:1-10; When Hannah sang unto the Lord her God.

"And Hannah prayed, and said, My heart rejoiceth in the Lord, mine horn is exalted in the Lord: my mouth is enlarged over mine

enemies; because I rejoice in thy salvation. There is none holy as the Lord: for there is none beside thee: neither is there any rock like our God. Talk no more so exceeding proudly; let not arrogance come out of your mouth: for the Lord is a God of knowledge, and by him, actions are weighed. (1 Samuel 2:1-3)

The book of Psalms is known for its poetic characteristics and is composed of several prayers and songs. Let us look at some of them.

"My heart is not proud, Lord, my eyes are not haughty; I do not concern myself with great matters or things too wonderful for me. But I have calmed and quieted myself, I am like a weaned the child with its mother; with a weaned child I am content. Israel, put your hope in the Lord both now and forevermore. Psalm 131 (KJV)

"I will praise you, Lord, with all my heart; before the "gods" I will sing your praise. I will bow down towards your holy temple and will praise your name for your unfailing love and your faithfulness, for you have so exalted solemn decree that it surpasses your fame. When I called, you answered me; you greatly emboldened me. May the kings of the earth praise you, Lord, when they hear what you have decreed. May they sing in the way of the Lord. For the glory of the Lord is great. (Psalm 138:1-5)

Prayers that get Results

As it is written in Matthew 21-22, if we have faith as a mustard seed, we can speak to any mountain, and the mountain will have to be removed, and cast into the sea, and they must obey because we speak the word of faith in Jesus Name.

Say it with authority:

- I command every mountain standing in the way of my life, be thou removed in Jesus' Name.

- I command every mountain that stands in the way of my family, be thou removed.

- I command every mountain standing in the way of my children, be thou removed.

- I command every mountain standing in the way of my finances, be thou remove in the Mighty Name of Jesus.
- I speak to every mountain that stands in the way of my career be paralyzed now.

- I speak to every mountain that stands in the way of my purpose, be removed now.

- I speak to every mountain that stands in the way of my destiny; be thou remove in Jesus Mighty Name.

- I command every mountain that stands in the way of my health, your time is up, be paralyzed and burnt to ashes in Jesus' Name.

- You mountain of disappointment, die by fire.

- You mountain of neglect, die by fire.

- You mountain of disgrace, die by fire.

- You mountain of low self-esteem, die by fire.

- You mountain of failure, die by fire.

- You mountain of poverty, die by fire.

- You mountain of bandage, die by fire.

- You mountain of lack, die by fire.

- You mountain of abuse, your time is up. Go now.

- You mountain of demonic oppression, leave my life now, in Jesus Mighty Name.

- You mountain of demonic harassment, catch fire.

- You mountain, of satanic interception, catch fire.

- I release fire and thunder upon every mountain of demonic implantation in Jesus' Name.

- May every mountain that has been set to destroy my marriage catch fire now.

- Every demon associated with problems, die by fire.
- Every demonic spirit plotting circumstance to bring us down, catch fire.

- I declare that no mountain will stand in my way in Jesus' Name

- I am unstoppable in Christ, and His blood will destroy all mountains standing in my way.

- I speak to the mountain of pride, die by fire.

- Let every cursed mountain, receive Holy Ghost Fire

- I speak to every spell-bound mountain. Your time is up. Die by fire, in the Mighty Name of Jesus.

CHAPTER 5

Positioning Ourselves in Prayer

There are different ways in which we can position ourselves to pray.

1. *Kneeling (Ezra 9:5, Daniel 6:10, Acts 20:36)*

Kneeling to pray has been practiced for centuries. People believe that the origin of kneeling to pray is derived from the practice of kneeling before kings and petitioning a request. This tradition symbolized humility and honor when going before a king or ruler. As believers, we approach God kneeling in prayer, in recognition and honor to Him as our sovereign King.

Throughout the Bible, we see where men and women of God would kneel to pray before Yahweh; it was their daily routine to seek the face of God by kneeling in surrender to God. On other occasions, they would go to God kneeling whenever they had a need.

In Ezra chapter 9, the princes came to Ezra and told him that the priests and the Levites had not separated themselves from the people of the nations, even of the Canaanites, the Hittites, the Perizzites, the Jebusites, the Ammonites, the Moabites, the Egyptians, and the Amorites. They took care of their daughters for themselves and their sons, so the holy seed mingled with the people of the land. When Ezra heard all this, he rented his garment and mantle, plucked off the hair of his head and beard, and sat down astonished. "And at the evening sacrifice I arose up from my heaviness; and having rent my garment and mantle, I fell upon my knees, and spread out my hands unto the Lord my God, and said, O my God, I am ashamed and blush to lift up my face to thee, my God: for our iniquities are increased over our head, and our trespass is grown up into the heavens." (Ezra 9:1-5).

The Bible also records prophets like Daniel kneeling in prayer. When Darius, the King of Persia took over the Kingdom from Babylon, he decided to divide the kingdom into 120 provinces and appointed a high officer to rule over each region. Daniel and two others were elected administrators to supervise the high officers and protect the king's interests. We see where Daniel proved himself more capable than all the other administrators and high officers because of his excellent skills and incredible ability that he was promoted. This caused jealousy toward Daniel, and the presidents and princes sought to create an occasion against him concerning the kingdom. They could not find a fault in Daniel but were persistent in their plight." All the presidents of the kingdom, the governors, and the princes, the counselors, and the captains, consulted together to establish a royal statute, to make a firm decree, that whosoever shall ask a petition of any God or man for thirty days, except to him the king, must be cast into the den of the Lion. They asked the King to establish a decree and sign the writing that it cannot be changed according to the laws of Medes Persians, which cannot be altered, and the king signed the writing and the decree. When Daniel knew all about this, and that the writing was signed, he went into his house; and his windows were open in his chamber towards Jerusalem, he knelt upon his knees three times a day, and prayed, and gave thanks before his God. (Daniel 6:1-10).

Altogether, servant leaders of the Lord and other Christians mostly kneel to pray whenever a serious situation occurs, and God's divine intervention is sought suddenly and supernaturally. These are often detrimental to our lives or the lives of others.

2. *Lying Down on a bed (Psalm 63:6)*
Lying down on a bed or couch is a more tranquil way to pray. In these cases, it could be that you forgot to pray before going to bed, woke up in the night, and prayed, or while sleeping,

the Spirit of the Lord woke you up, and in obedience, you begin to pray while lying in bed.

There were many times when I was sleeping, and the Holy Spirit woke me up to pray, either because the enemy launched an attack or someone was going through a challenging situation, and I needed to intercede. On other occasions, I had terrible dreams where demonic powers confronted me, and I woke up and started praying immediately.

A relaxing mood is easily created when we lay prostrate in prayer. This posture facilitates deep meditation on God's word, presence, power, and Kingdom. This atmosphere is generally ideal for reflecting on God's faithfulness in prayer with thanksgiving. If you surveyed Christians, they would tell you that weeping before God is usually automatic whenever they're lying down in prayer, causing their pillows and sheets to become soaked in tears. We will go into this further into the reading. "I lie awake thinking of you, meditating on you through the night" Psalm 63:6 (NLT).

Whenever our minds are on the Lord, we will go to bed praying and wake up doing the same; we may even question whether we got enough sleep because the Lord consumes our minds.

Some persons may prefer this position in prayer because of its comfort and convenience, while others might be too lazy to change their posture. Whatever the reason, it will be effective once the prayer is offered with the right motive and is sincere.

3.*Sitting (1 Chronicles 17:16)*

Sitting while praying is just as potent as the other positions. It is a comfortable and relaxing posture like lying down, but this doesn't imply that little effort is required in practice.

When I pray sitting, I usually reflect on all the things God had done for me, how He miraculously provided, blowing my mind with His faithfulness, and the many times He delivered me from the schemes of the adversary by rescuing me when I could not save myself.

When I sit and think about the awesomeness of God and where He has brought me from, I often cry in awe before the Lord. The truth is, I am conscious that I did not do anything to deserve all that God has done for me, and I find peace in expressing myself to him in prayer. This may be common among believers who, in reflection, cannot help but give God thanks, praise, and commune constantly through prayer.

In the bible we read of King David when he went in and sat before the Lord and said, who am I, O Lord God, and what is my house and family, that You have brought me up to this? 1 Chronicles 17:16 (KJV)

Even David, when he was confronted by the Prophet Nathan with the word of God, sat down and reflected on God's goodness and mercies. Sometimes we receive a word from God that cuts so deep within us that we can't help but think about it.

As a minister of the gospel, there are times when I sit as I reflect and make preparation to carry out an assignment. I usually relax and think about the Holy Spirit and the remarkable presence of God. Even when traveling, whether by plane or vehicle, I find it easy to take time to meditate and seek God through prayer. Others may sit and do the same at their offices, on their lunch break, or at any time made available as each day progresses.

4. *Standing (1 Kings 8:22, Nehemiah 9:4-5)*
Standing is the most radical of all the different positions while praying. This position is assumed whenever there is cooperative prayer, sometimes for hours. People are more charged and ready whenever they're standing and praying. You may find that many believers are more comfortable in

this position because they are less likely to be distracted, and it is challenging for anyone to become sleepy. The general environment where this posture is practiced is during a church service or an outdoor meeting.

Have you ever seen a believer very mad with the devil because of something that occurred? Maybe there was a spiritual attack in their family or workplace, and they decided to fight back against the enemy by praying. In these circumstances, the person will only take a standing position and pray radically. One can therefore deduce that warfare prayers are primarily associated with standing.

There is something about standing and praying whenever the devil wages war against the people of God or something terrible has happened to a believer. Whenever there is a dire situation, and we need God's divine intervention suddenly, the position that most people go into to pray is standing. It's like it pushes our war button to go off into fighting the enemy. Many of you can attest to this because we are people of war and cannot expect to be anything different, in truth, our Father is the God of war.

"And they stood in their place and read from the Book of the Law of the Lord their God for a fourth of the day, and for another fourth of it they confessed and worshiped the Lord their God. On the stairs of the Levites stood Jeshua, Bani, Kadmiel, Shebaniah,

Bunni, Sherebiah, Bani, and Chenani, and they cried with a loud voice to the Lord their God. Then the Levites Jeshua, Kadmiel, Bani, Hashabneiah, Sherebiah, Hodiah, Shebaniah, and Pethahiah said, stand up and bless the Lord your God from everlasting to everlasting. Blessed be Your glorious name which is exalted above all blessing and praise." Nehemiah 9:3-5 (KJV)

5. *Bowing to the ground (Exodus 34: 8, Psalm 95:6)*
To bow down to someone or something means to show weakness by agreeing to the demands or following the orders of (someone or something). Psalm 95:6 declares, "Oh come, let us worship and bow down; let us kneel before the Lord, our Maker!"

"So that the name of Jesus every knee should bow, in heaven and on earth and under the earth." (Philippians 2:10)

"For this reason, I bow my knees before the Father..." Ephesians 3:14 Bowing before God is not just about kneeling, which was mentioned earlier. When we bow before our King, it demonstrates His Sovereignty and Superiority over us and reveals our inadequacy, weaknesses, and vulnerability without God. Our susceptibility as we bow in submission reflects our complete trust in God to bring an urgent resolution to the matters arising when we lack the endurance to cope.

When we carefully observe the children of Israel's lives and behavior in the Old Covenant, especially in the book of Judges 2:10, the Bible tells us that after Joshua's death and Generation, another generation arose. They knew not the Lord nor the works he had done for Israel, so they did evil in the sight of God and followed other gods. Everyone did what seemed right in their own eyes, and whenever they sinned, God would deliver them into the hands of their enemies. However, when their pain was too much to bear, they would go before God, bow down, repent and cry before Him. When they did this, God would hear their cry and raise a Judge to deliver them out of the hands of their enemies.

We can say then that bowing before God has a strong sense of urgency and desperation. Whenever the people of God bow before Him, they require an immediate answer, a desperate move of His presence, or divine intervention for a severe crisis beyond human control.

It is so beautiful to see the people of God bowing in worship and adoration; we can fall at the master's feet and magnify His name.

6. *Lying on the ground (2 1Samuel 12:16, Matthew 26: 39)*
Another interesting position in praying is lying on the floor. What makes this unique and fascinating is that it is not the

most comfortable place to be because the surface is hard. Remember that you're not lying-in bed; stop and think for a moment. You may ask, what are some reasons a person or persons would want to use this position in prayer?

There can be several reasons to include the following:

- Crying to God over a situation you need an urgent answer for and refusing to get up until a response is granted.

Have you ever experienced someone close to you dying suddenly in an unexpected way and could not understand why they died? Maybe I can relate more to those in ministry who have dedicated their time, energy, and entire life to the church, making countless sacrifices for the Kingdom of God. While engaged doing the work of God, if met with a tragedy in their family, the first move is usually to fall on their face before God as they seek answers to the questions bombarding their minds.

We see how David sinned against God when he killed Uriah in battle, took his wife, and got her pregnant. The Bible tells us that God sent Nathan, the prophet, to David. After their conversation, Nathan returns home, but we see David in a vulnerable state. Nathan returned to his house, and the Lord sent a deadly illness to the child of David and Uriah's wife. David went before God lying on the bare ground without food all night, begging God to spare the child's life, when he found out that his child was going to die. (2 Samuel 12:15-16)

- People also lay flat on the ground whenever they're engaged in an intense fast.

Personally, whenever I am desperate to get closer to God and desire a profound revelation or insight into something, I would typically go on my belly in an intense fast before the Lord. I believe that I dig deeper into God, into the realm of the supernatural and miraculous, and reach higher heights in prayer whenever I go before God on my belly, pressing desperately.

6. *Lifting holy hands towards heaven*
   (1 Timothy 2:8, Psalm 28:2, Isaiah 1:15)

Praying and lifting our hands are typical actions in prayer that are expressed naturally. A part of us always wants to worship God, and because we are worshiping beings, it is tough for our hands to stay down or still whenever we pray. 1 Timothy 2:8 speaks about the attitude of men in prayer, which should be pursued as a lifestyle as we pray and lift our hands to the Almighty in reverence and surrender. It is always beautiful to see the people of God praying and raising their hands in surrendering to the King of all Kings, recognizing His power, dominion, and authority. God is Sovereign, and His name must be always lifted, whether we feel to do it or not; we have a duty and responsibility to pray. The psalmist in Psalm 28:2 was crying out to God for mercy and help. "Hear the voice of my supplications, when I cry unto thee, when I lift up my hands toward thy holy oracle." By reading the passage, we could feel the desperate cry for God's divine intervention in the situation at hand.

Most times, the lifting of hands while praying takes place during a service where the people of God gather for fellowship. Believers raise their hands when a special prayer request is honored, during regular prayer, praise, or declarations.

I find praying and lifting hands very interesting because whenever I do the same, I simply thank God for His response to the requests I am praying about, intensifying my praise to the Father. God loves a heart of gratitude. Whenever we enter His presence with a heart of gratitude, He will move on our behalf because we are simply expressing our appreciation for all He has done for us and all He has allowed us to go through.

The Power to Win Prayer

As it is written, "If we pray according to the will of God, we will always get the results we need in prayer." (1 John 5:14)

- I declare that all my prayers will be in line with God's perfect will in Jesus' Name; I declare that self will be crucified.

- I pray that my ego and emotions are subjected to the power of the Holy Spirit so that I will not pray amiss.

- I declare that my understanding will be open as I study the word of God.

- I declare that the mystery of the Kingdom will be revealed to me through prayer in the Name of Jesus.

- Lord, cause me to understand things kept as a secret before the foundation of the world.

As it is written in Psalm 1, I declare that I will not walk in the counsel of the ungodly, nor stand in the way of sinners, or be seated in the seat of the scornful. I declare that I will take great pleasure in the word of God and meditate upon it day and night. I shall be like a tree, planted by the rivers of water that bring forth fruit in his season, my leaf will not wither, and whatsoever I do will prosper in the Mighty Name of Jesus.

CHAPTER 6

Prayers for the Manifestation of Miracles

"For as the rain cometh down, and the snow from heaven, and returneth not thither, but watereth the earth, and maketh it bring forth and bud, that it may give seed to the sower, and bread to the eater, so shall my word be that goeth forth out of my mouth: it shall not return to me void, but it shall accomplish that which I please, and it shall prosper in the thing whereto I sent it." (Isaiah 55:10-11)

As it is written, every God-designed word spoken over my life and destiny shall come to pass in Jesus' name.
I declare that the word of the Lord shall take root and bring forth countless miracles in my life in the mighty name of Jesus.

- I declare that I will be everything that the word of God said I am, and nothing will change or stop that in Jesus' mighty name.

- I declare that the word of God will break and destroy every restriction to my financial breakthrough in the powerful name of Jesus Christ of Nazareth.

- May everything that opposes the word of God for my life die by fire!

- Let every demonic spirit sent to stop the manifestation of God's word in my life catch fire now in Jesus' Mighty name, I pray.

- I declare that whatever the word of God says shall come to pass.

- Through the power of God's word, let everything that stands in the way of my miracles receive thunder.

- Through the power of God's word, let every demonic concentration receive the lightning of God now, in the name of Jesus.

- I declare that the spoken word of God will break through every impenetrable wall in Jesus' Mighty name, I pray.
- Let the atmosphere over my life change from defeat to victory, in Jesus' name.
- Let the atmosphere over my life change from poverty to prosperity, in the powerful name of Jesus.

- May the atmosphere of disappointment in my life change to divine appointment, favor, and success.

- By the power of God's word, I declare that there will be no more confusion and restriction in the atmosphere around me.

- I command the atmosphere to submit to God's power, authority, and will concerning my life in the powerful name of Jesus.

- I declare that money will locate me.

- I declare that the fire of God has paralyzed the spirit of delay. Everything that has been delayed in my life shall manifest now by the power of the word.

- By the power of the Holy Spirit, I command everything that stands in the way of my miracles to die by fire.

- By the power of the blood of Jesus, I command every illegal operation taking place in my life to receive the lightning of God in Jesus' powerful name.

- I declare that I shall not die in poverty.
- I declare that I shall not die poor.

- I declare that neither I nor my children and spouse shall die prematurely in Jesus' Name.

- By the word of the Lord, I command every curse over my life to be broken with immediate effects in the name of Jesus Christ

- Generational curses break and lose your hold on my life and my children and loved ones.

- lineage curse, break and lose your grip on my life, children, and loved ones.

- ancestral curse, break and lose your hold on my life in Jesus' mighty name.

- By the power of the word of God, I command the:

  - ✓ spell of the enemy to be broken now from my life.

  - ✓ spell of sickness, break by fire

  - ✓ spell of low self-esteem, be broken by fire

  - ✓ spell of abortion, break by fire
  - ✓ the spell of adultery

- ✓ spell of immorality

- ✓ spell of murder

- ✓ spell of lies

- ✓ spell of malice

- ✓ spell of witchcraft

- ✓ spell of poverty

- I command you to lose your hold on my life and die by fire in the name of Jesus.

Types of Prayers

1. Prayer of Request/Petition

People regularly use this type of prayer; both save and unsaved. This is popular because many have been cultured to believe that prayer is all about asking. The truth is, we are always in need of something, and we know the best person to ask for things is Jesus.

In John 17:15, Jesus gave us a perfect example of a prayer of request/ supplication before ascending into heaven. He prayed to God the Father and asked him to keep the disciples in the world and protect them from the evil one.

Other passages in the Bible provide examples of a prayer of request.

Matthew 21:22 (AMP) declares, "whatever you ask for in prayer, having faith and believing, you will receive."

After challenging the false prophets, Elijah prayed a prayer of request when he was on Mount Carmel. Four hundred and fifty prophets of Baal and four hundred prophets of Asherah ate at Jezebel's table. After Elijah had allowed the false prophets to make their altar and present their sacrifices, they called on their god (Baal) from morning until noon, even cutting themselves, but nothing happened. Elijah then repaired the altar, presented his sacrifice, and called upon his God, Jehovah. He used these words: "Lord God of Abraham, Isaac, and Israel, let it be known this day, that thou art God in Israel, and that I am your servant, and that I have done all these things at thy word. Hear me, O Lord, hear me, that these people may know that thou art the Lord God and that thou hast turned their hearts back again." (1 Kings 18:17-38).

The God we serve is very loving and merciful, slow to anger, and always abounding in love (Psalm 103:8). Even when we sin against God, and His wrath is turned towards us to destroy us, he will remove his anger and give us another chance if we cry out to him sincerely. We see a perfect example of this in Isaiah 38:1-5. When king Hezekiah was sick unto death, God sent the prophet Isaiah to tell him to get his house in order, and he shall die and not live. Hezekiah then turned his face towards the wall, prayed unto the Lord, and cried out for mercy. The Lord answered his prayer and sent Isaiah to tell him that He (God) had added fifteen years to his life.

Like the prophets and even you are reading, I have prayed the prayer of request many times in my life. Frankly, it may be the most regular prayer I have prayed, along with the prayer of thanksgiving. Let's face reality; we are always in situations where we need God to do something for us. As for me, I know that I am vulnerable and weak without God's help in my life. There was never a time when I operated without requesting that God do something for me or someone else.

As a child of God, I am conscious and confident that God can grant us the desires of our hearts if it is in line with His will. Let's pause for reflection; what better person to go to with our requests or petitions other than God? Remember that He is our eternal Father, Rock, Refuge, and Strength.

God will never turn His back on us whenever we approach Him with our needs.

Isaiah 59:1 declares, "Behold, the Lord's hands are not shortened, that it cannot save; neither his ear heavy, that he cannot hear. Our loving, great, compassionate and kind father God, knows our petitions before we even come to him, God knows everything about us, he knows our needs, desires and passions."

2. *Prayer of Thanksgiving*

The book of Psalms is filled with prayers of thanksgiving. As the name suggests, this prayer excludes making requests and focuses on giving thanks. Believers approach the Master with a heart of gratitude for all he has done in the past. Reflection on God's blessing and extended mercies are paramount in showing this appreciation to God the Father for his:

- *Divine protection* – words aren't enough to tell God thanks for all he has protected us from, is protecting us from, and will continue to protect us from.

- *Divine provision* – all we need, God has already provided for us. He is our "Jehovah Jireh."

- *Divine restoration* – there are so many things God has restored in our lives repeatedly.

- *Divine comfort* – how often has God comforted us when we were broken, hurt, rejected, forsaken, abused, neglected, depressed, confused, sick, etc.? God has always been there for us, and we can always lean and cry on His shoulder.

- *Divine peace* – the peace of God has always been there for us. Our minds are often suppressed by many issues and thoughts that could have driven us crazy. Amid this reality, the peace of God always comes to our rescue.

Paul urged the church at Colossae to "Be earnest and undesired and steadfast in prayer and be alert and intent in thanksgiving." (Colossians 4:2 AMP)

In Psalm 95:1-4, we see the expression of gratitude and praise, "O Come let us sing unto the Lord: let us make a joyful noise to the rock of our salvation. Let us come before his presence with thanksgiving and make a joyful noise unto him with psalms. For the Lord is a great God, and a great King above all God's. In his hand are the deep places of the earth."

3. *Prayer of Desperation*

The name speaks for itself. The moment someone hears the word desperation, they know there is a need for urgent intervention. Being desperate is characterized by a state of despair or distress, where a person feels hopeless and requires divine intervention.

There must be a situation in the person's life that they are unable to deal with, and, as such, a solution is sought to escape. It doesn't matter who you are, your race, skin complexion, family background, or even your accomplishments in life. Once you're a human being, there will come a time in your life when you face a situation you cannot deal with or overcome yourself. When this happens, you will need the aid of someone else. The condition can sometimes be overwhelming or burdensome, with the propensity to cause depression and catapult us into panic mode. If not careful, we may seek assistance in the wrong places or from the wrong set of people. The easiest time to make bad decisions is when people are in desperate situations. Remember now that whenever you want to rid yourself of something, the desire is always great to do whatever it takes to get to a solution.

Being desperate can come in many different forms. It can come from a state of abuse where a person has been exploited for years and find themselves at a breaking point. The feeling of 'enough is enough' will always see the victim seeking help to move away from their abuser. It is essential to know that abuse may take different forms, whether verbally, physically, emotionally, or even psychologically, and is not only limited to private/family relationships. Sometimes this is spiraled from the work environment and other outside interactions. Can you think about any time in your life when you needed protection and rescue from something or someone? Those who face abuse and desire a way of escape usually become thirsty for protection and deliverance. If you or someone you know is going through abuse and requires help, reach out to someone today.

Many people have found themselves in situations that cause them to pray a prayer of desperation. The children of Israel encountered a situation where three nations came against them: Ammon, Moab, and mount Seir. The truth is, one of these nations could have destroyed Judah because each nation had more fighting men and weapons. If Judah was no match for one of these nations, how could they defeat three? They had to face a reality that mirrored that of a giant versus an ant in battle. Jehoshaphat was the king of Judah during the time and heard about the threats of the three nations. He became very fearful and sought the Lord, then called a fast throughout all of Judah. People came from every city of Judah to seek the Lord. While praying and telling God that they have no power to go against the enemy, Jehoshaphat makes a profound statement; "neither knows what to do: but our eyes are upon thee." As soon as King Jehoshaphat finishes praying in his despair, God sends Jahaziel to encourage him not to be afraid or dismayed because the battle is not his but the Lord's. God did fight the war; Judah went out for battle with the Levis, leading and singing praises to God, and God set ambushment against Ammon, Moab, and Mount Seir.

No matter who we are or what we go through, God is faithful to help us in our cry for help. Even the thief on the cross prayed a prayer of desperation to Jesus, asking Jesus to remember him, and Jesus replied, "today you will be with me in paradise."

4. Covenant Prayer
A covenant is a written agreement or promise usually under seal between two or more parties and signifies a contract, commitment, pledge, or promise. When someone makes a covenant, it is a lifetime agreement, which should not be broken. Throughout the bible, we see where God made a covenant with His people and vice versa. A covenant is good but can be challenging, especially in extreme cases where lives may be at stake. The commitment helps build accountability and responsibility.

Samson prayed this kind of prayer when he became blind, was chained by the Philistine, and placed in the house. "And Samson called unto the Lord, and said, Lord God, remember me, I pray there, and strengthen me, I pray there, only once, O God, that I may be at once avenged of the Philistine for my two eyes." Judges 16:28

After Samson had finished praying, he took hold of the middle pillars upon which the house stood and on which it was borne up, of the one with his right hand and of the other with his left. (Judges 1628-29)

We also see Hannah praying the covenant prayer at her breaking point for a miracle. After being barren for a very long time, her rival Peninnah would provoke her day and night because they both shared the same husband, and she gave birth to children, but Hannah couldn't because the Lord had closed her womb. Hannah would not eat for days, and she would go to the Temple and wept before the Lord.
"So, Hannah rose up after they had eaten in Shiloh, and after they had drunk. Now Eli the priest sat upon a seat by a post of the Temple of the Lord. And she was in bitterness of soul, and prayed unto the Lord, and wept. And she vows, and said, O Lord of hosts, if thou wilt indeed look on the affliction of thine handmade, and remember me, and not forget thine handmade, but wilt give unto thine handmade a man child,

then I will give him unto the Lord all the days of his life, and there shall be no razor come upon his head. And it came to pass, as she continued praying before the Lord, that Eli marked her mouth. Now Hannah, she spoke from her heart; only her lips moved, but her voice was not heard therefore, Eli thought she had been drunk." (1Samuel 1:9-13)

Many today love to pray but do not bother to fulfill their vows. When someone is in trouble and can't find a way out, the most accessible name to call is "Jesus." A famous quotation for a safe person in crisis is, "Lord, if you get me out of this situation, I promise you that I will give my heart to you for the rest of my life." How many unsaved people fulfilled this vow after committing to it in trouble? Unfortunately, many are living with that guilt today.

The bible constantly reminds us that God is merciful and loving, so when we cry out to Him for help, He will help us. Like the unsaved who have made a vow to commit to an authentic relationship with God, Several Christians have found themselves in situations that only the divine intervention of God could relieve them.

The situation could be a marital collapse where one party decides to leave after many years because they feel it's time for a change or bankruptcy arising from losing a job. In this case, the bills may be excessive, and possessions (house, car, credit cards, etc.) may be on the verge of being lost. Other general instances may include an unfaithful or unsuccessful relationship. Still, the person is struggling because they desire marriage or have faced a serious court case where the border between imprisonment and freedom is faint. In despair, the individual may seek God's help while pledging a commitment to do something for Him.

These are some frequent situations that cause people to pray the covenant prayer.

There are different instances where people prayed the covenant prayer. For example, a dedicated believer desiring more of God and His presence would pray this prayer as they choose to work for God in winning souls and leading His people on the right path. I often pray the covenant prayer. My conversations with God would usually include, "Lord, if You entrust me with Your presence in an unusual way, prepare me, and allow the FRUIT of the Spirit to be in full operation in my life, I will do anything for the Kingdom." I also ask that the GIFTS of the Spirit be supernaturally manifested in my life. And seek for the Spirit of "REVELATION" and "WISDOM" to rest upon me all the days of my life. After asking, I commit to ensuring that I win His Kingdom as many souls as possible. I will be a "Weapon" of mass destruction to the kingdom of Satan. I will remain humble and give all the glory to my master.

5. Prayer of Deliverance

The prayer of deliverance is like the prayer of covenant; the only difference is the absence of a vow to God to secure His help. The master of this kind of prayer is King David. David was a man after God's own heart, possessing a unique and special relationship with Him. He knew how to entertain God with singing and music. He loved God with all of his heart and danced in His presence until his garment fell off. David didn't care who saw and thought that he, being king, was going crazy in worship; he knew the mind and heart of God. He also knew where to find Him. David was filled with God and love for Him. He prayed with certainty because he knew God would come through for him.

Throughout the Psalms, we see David asking the Lord for deliverance.

Psalm 72:12 (NLT) – He will rescue the poor when they cry to him; he will help the oppressed, who have no one to defend them.

Psalm 22:1-6 (AMP) – My God, My God, why have you forsaken me? Why are you so far from helping me, and from the words of my groaning? O my God, I cried in the daytime, but You answer not; and by night I am not silent or find no rest. But You are holy, O You Who dwell in (the holy place where) the praises of Israel (are offered). Our fathers trusted in You; they trusted (leaned on, relied on You, and were confident) and You delivered them. They cried to You and were delivered; they trusted in, leaned on, and confidently relied on You, and were not ashamed or confused or disappointed. But I am a worm, and no man; I am the scorn of men and despised by the people."

Psalm 34:18 (AMP) – The Lord is close to those who are of a broken heart and save such as are crushed with sorrow for sin and are humbly and thoroughly patient.

Psalm 34:19 (AMP) – Many evils confront the (consistency) righteous, but the Lord delivers him out of them all.

As believers, we must always be conscious that God has ears and takes pleasure in delivering his people. At no point in time will God allow the enemy to defeat us. The key to our deliverance is to "cry" out to the Lord. To cry is to shed tears, especially as an expression of distress or pain. In extreme circumstances, it may be a shout or scream to express one's fear, pain, or grief.

When situations are at their lowest, there is nothing else to do but call on the only one who can help. You will find added strength and energy in God as you call out to him in your misery. The magnitude of your pain will determine the level of intensity of your cry. The Children of Israel were in bondage in Egypt for about four hundred years. Pharaoh had them doing hard labor and had his slave drivers abuse and oppress them daily. After many years of abuse and mistreatment, the people of God decided that enough was enough. They remembered that they had the only one true wise God, whose name was YAHWEH.

"And they cried out to the Lord in their misery, and their cries went up to God. God heard their groaning, and he remembered his covenant with Abraham, with Isaac and with Jacob. So, God looked at the Israelites and was concerned about them." (Exodus 2:24-25)

After hearing the cry of his people (the Israelites), God reacts by appearing to Moses at the burning bush. He expressed himself to Moses and told him about the condition of His people whom he was chosen to deliver. The Lord said, "I have indeed seen the misery of my people in Egypt. I have heard them crying out because of their slave drivers, and I am concerned about their suffering. So, I have come down to rescue them from the hand of the Egyptians and to bring them up out of the land into a good and spacious land, a land flowing with milk and honey. (Exodus 3:7-8)

It wasn't their situation that drew God's attention and pulled Him to rescue them. God already knew about their condition and all that was taking place in their lives; the intensity of their cry drew God's attention. There is something special about crying out in anguish, desperation, and sincerity of heart unto God. This kind of cry reaches God the most and pulls him to intervene in our lives.

As you're reading this book, what kind of situation are you facing? Where do you need God to come and rescue you? He is the God of the suddenly and will save you from your situation. It doesn't matter how long you have been in it or how much effect it has had on you. God can arise in the lives of His people if they cry out to him.

One thing that causes many believers not to receive deliverance is pride, seeing yourself higher than you ought to be— believing more in your ability than in the power of God.

Many people allow pride to take hold of them that it blinds their eyes to the supernatural power of God. It is challenging to receive deliverance when overcome with pride. You may ask why? You rely entirely on your ability and wisdom with pride, blocking all other sources. The scripture declares that God does not walk with the proud nor scornful. If a person is prideful, they will not experience the full manifestation of God's grace.

Pride always comes before a fall. For this reason, many people died before being healed, some with unforgiveness in their hearts because they refused to give up pride.

Look at the life of the Syrophoenician woman, whose daughter was possessed by an evil spirit. She heard about Jesus and all He had done and was doing, so she believed and sought-after Him. When she came to Jesus and begged that the demon be cast out of her daughter (keep in mind that she didn't ask, but begged), Jesus replied, "First let the children eat all they want," "For it is not right to take the children's bread and toss it to their dogs." What Jesus was simply saying to her is that he came for the Jews first, and the gospel is first for the Jews, so it is not right to give healing to other nations and people, who are not God's chosen people.   (Mark 7:24-30)

You would have thought by now that the woman would have gotten upset and given up by Jesus' response, but instead, she humbled herself before the Lord and said, "Yes, Lord," "But even the dogs under the table eat the children's crumbs." Then Jesus told her, "For such a reply; you may go;

the demon has left your daughter." She returned and found her daughter lying on the bed and the demon was gone. People of a humble heart and spirit are most likely to receive a miracle from God.

There is a fascinating story in the Bible that speaks about the cry for deliverance. Jesus went to Jericho with his disciples, together with a large crowd; they were leaving the city, and a blind man named Bartimaeus (that is, the son of Timaeus) was sitting at the roadside begging. When he heard that it was Jesus of Nazareth passing by, the blind man began to shout, "Jesus, Son of David, have mercy on me!" Many of those in the crowd rebuked him and told him to be quiet, but the more they tried to shut him up, the more he began to shout, "Jesus Son of David, have mercy on me!" (Mark 10:46-47)

You know what happens when someone cries out to Jesus for help; he is touched by the cry and will react. When the blind man cried out to Jesus He stopped and said, "Call him." So the same people rebuking the blind man earlier called him and told him to "Cheer up! On your feet, He's calling you." The blind man then jumped to his feet and came to Jesus, Jesus then asked him a question, "What do you want me to do for you?" Jesus replied, blind Bartimaeus quickly replied, "Rabbi (Teacher), I want to see." Then Jesus said, "Go, your

faith has healed you." And immediately he received his sight.
Mark 10:48–52

6. *Prayer of Confession and Repentance*
Many Christians today do not know the difference between confession and repentance. When a pastor preaches and receives a word from the Lord for the congregation to repent of their sins, the response is merely a repeat of the statement, "Lord, I repent," but are they saying, "Lord, I confess?" Are they telling God they are sorry? This has been a noticeable pattern since I started serving in ministry. Unfortunately, several church leaders do not understand their differences or proper usage. It could be that they weren't taught and, upon reading the scriptures, did not get the interpretation by the Holy Spirit.

Though the two words function concurrently, they are different. Confession is a written or spoken statement expressing that you have done something wrong or committed a crime. Its Greek word "homologous," pronounced homologeo means to acknowledge, admit, declare, or agree fully to something.

Homologous presents two implications when we examine deeply into it. Let's dissect it together.

- *Homo* – is a Latin word that means man or human

When used as a prefix, as in "homosexual," it derives from the Greek word homos which denotes the same.

- *Logos* – is Greek for "word."

In the first chapter of St John, Jesus is identified as "The Word," incarnated or made flesh.

When we put the two together, we derive a man or human, acknowledging with words (the word), admitting using words (the word), and declaring using words (the word). Before approaching the throne of grace, we must first recognize and acknowledge that we have sinned against God and need cleansing. No sin can enter or stay in the presence of God because God is too pure to look at sin; sin sicks His stomach.

Being pure and holy, God will exclusively react to things that are pure, having fellowship only with those who are holy. If we fail to acknowledge that we have sinned as the scripture said or have no sin, we deceive ourselves, and the truth is not in us. *If we say we have not sinned, we make him a liar, and his word is not in us.). If we confess our sins, he is faithful and just to forgive us our sins and cleanse us from all unrighteousness. (1 John 1:8-10)*

David was known for confessing. He would always go before the Lord broken and seek forgiveness.

"I acknowledge my sin to You, and my iniquity did not hide. I said, I will confess my transgressions to the Lord (continually unfolding the past till all is told) – then You (instantly) forgave me the guilt and iniquity of my sin. (Pause, and calmly think of that)." Psalm 32:5

God knows everything about us. He knows our beginning from the end, God numbers even the hair on our heads. His eyes go to and from the earth, beholding the good and the evil. It is best for us to be true to ourselves, best when we come to ourselves, and not under pretence.

The psalmist was right when he said, "O Lord, you have examined my heart and know everything about me. You know when I sit or stand up. You know my thoughts even when I'm far away. You see me when I travel and when I rest at home. You know everything I do. You know what I am going to say even before I say it, Lord. You go before me and follow me. You place your hand of blessing on my head. I can never escape from your Spirit! I can never get away from your presence! If I go up to heaven, you are there; if I go down to the grave, you are there. If I ride the wings of the morning, if I dwell by the farthest oceans, even there your hand will guide me, and your strength will support me. I could ask the darkness to hide me and the light to become night, but even in darkness I cannot hide from you. To you the night shines as bright as day. Darkness and light are the same to you. (Psalm 139:1-12 NLT)

Confession has two stages:

- Confession of the heart.
- Confession of the mouth.

Confession of the heart
Confession first begins in our hearts. The heart is the central and inner awareness of our body or being. When the Bible speaks of the "heart," it does not refer to our physical organs that pump blood throughout the body but to the whole of man's intellect, emotion, and will.

"And He said, what comes out of a man is what makes a man unclean and renders (him) unhallowed. For within, (that is) out of the hearts of men, come base and wicked thoughts, sexual immorality, stealing, murder, adultery. Coveting (a greedy desire to have more wealth), dangerous and destructive wickedness, deceit; u restrained (indecent) conduct; an evil eye (envy), slander (evil speaking, malicious misrepresentation, abusiveness), pride (the sin of an uplifted heart against God and man), foolishness (folly, lack of sense, recklessness, thoughtlessness). All these evil (purposes and desires) come from within, and they make the man unclean and render him unhallowed." Mark 7:20-23 (AMP)

A person must first admit, believe, and acknowledge that he has sinned against God and hurt God's feelings. Whenever you hurt someone in a relationship, a void (gap) is created, which is unhealthy. There is a parallel to our relationship with God; the Bible says that we sin in our very thoughts and deeds. David placed Uriah at the front of a battle to be killed, to have Bathsheba. He took her and got her pregnant. Though the child died, David sinned against God.

When God sent Nathan the Profit to confront David, he became broken and cried out to the Lord from a broken heart and said these words.

Have mercy upon me, O God, according to your loving kindness: according unto the multitude of thy tender mercies blot out my transgressions. Wash me thoroughly from my iniquity, and cleanse me from my sin. For I acknowledge my transgressions: and my sin is ever before me. Against thee, thee only, have I sinned, and done this evil in thy sight: that thou mightest be justified when thou speakest, and be clear when thou judgest. Behold I was shapen in iniquity; and in sin did my mother conceive me. Behold, thou desirest truth in the inward parts: and in the hidden part thou shalt make me to know wisdom. Purge me with hyssop, and I shall be clean: wash me, and I shall be whiter than snow. Make me hear joy and gladness; that the bones which thou hast broken may rejoice. Hide their face from my sins and blot out all mine iniquities. "Great in me a clean heart, O God; and renew a right spirit without me. Cast me not away from the presence; and take not their holy Spirit from me. Restore unto me the joy of thy salvation; and uphold me with the free spirit". (Psalm 51:1-12)

Confession of the Mouth
"If thou shalt confess with the mouth the Lord Jesus and believe in thine heart that God raised him from the dead, thou shalt be saved. For with the heart man believeth unto righteousness; and with the mouth confession is made unto salvation." (Romans 10:9-10)

We must speak the word from our mouths because God desires to hear it. You cannot be telling someone you caused hurt, sorry silently as though you're humming. They deserve to hear it and know you're genuinely sorry for what you have done.

There are two kinds of Confessions.

- Confession to God
- Confession to Human

Most of the time, as Christians, we try our best to mend our broken relationship with God through confession. But how many of us stop to reflect on how we hurt not only God but also others? Just as God can be violated, hurt, and offended by our actions, so it is with the people around us, whether in church, school, or work environs. We often hurt each other but intentionally or unintentionally, we never confess, ignoring the persons feeling to talk to God about it.

Talking to God is good, but the person you hurt is still hurting. "How can you say that you love a God who you cannot see, and you can't love the person who you can see? You must first love the person who you see before you can love God. (1 John 4:20)

The scripture also expresses that we must confess our sins to each other and pray for each other so that we may be healed.

Therefore, confess your sins to one another [your false steps, your offenses], and pray for one another, that you may be healed and restored. The heartfelt and persistent prayer of a righteous man (believer) can accomplish much [when put into action and made effective by God—it is dynamic and can have tremendous power]. (James 5:16)

7. *Warfare/ Judgmental Prayer*

These are prayers Christians pray against their enemies. Our real enemy is the devil and his demons, but he uses people who availed themselves to be used by him. They aim to crack us in every way possible to kill us, stop our purpose, and prevent us from reaching our destiny.

From the Old Testament until now, the people of God have constantly been attacked or under attack. We must keep fighting to maintain our relationship with God and secure our souls for Christ's second coming.

Throughout the scriptures, we see where God's people would ask Him to defeat their enemies when under attack.

David was well known for these prayers because he had many enemies throughout his life, even from within his own house. Here are some examples:

"Content, O Lord, with those who contend with me; fight against those who fight me! Take hold of the shield and buckler and stand up for my help! Draw out also the spear and javelin and close up the way of those who pursue and prosecute me. Say to me, I am your deliverance! Let them be put to shame and dishonor who seek and require my life; let them be turned back and confused who plan my hurt! Let them be as chaff before the wind, with the Angel of the Lord driving them on." Psalm 35:1-5 (AMP)

"These wicked people are born sinners; even from birth they have lied and are together in their own way. They split venom like deadly snakes; they are like cobras that refuse to listen, ignoring the tunes of the snake chargers, no matter how skillfully they play. Break off their fangs, O Lord! Smash the jaw of these lions, O Lord! May they disappear like water into thirsty ground. Make their weapons useless in their hands." Psalm 58: 3-7 (NLT)

"Yea, though I walk through the valley of the shadow of death, I will fear no evil: for thou art with me; they rod and thy staff they comfort me." Psalm 23:4

As the Bible declares, there is a time and place for everything under the sun. Our enemies will go over the limits with us as believers with their efforts to wipe us out. We must stand up like warriors and fight back in prayer just as David did when his enemies were after him day and night.

We can't be friendly to the enemy; we must fight back with violent prayer whenever they attack. Our God is a God of war and has never lost a battle. When we summon heaven to respond and act on our behalf, we know without a shadow of a doubt that the God that answers by fire will come to our rescue. God has promised us in His word that he will never leave or forsake us, and that he is our very present help in times of trouble.

Contemporary society is filled with immense evil; there has never been a time on earth when iniquity was this rampant. People seem to be sporting evil with little to no fear of God in the hearts. People no longer respect the place of worship. We have seen several reports of shooters walking into churches and killing many people, including pastors and other leaders. Those of us whose eyes are open are aware that the individual or people carrying out these vicious acts are not the main culprits but the spirits working through them. The warfare we face as believers is very serious, and should not be underestimated because "the enemy, the devil, is out like a roaring lion seeking whom he may devour" (1 Peter 5:8). "But I thank God that he has given us power to tread upon scorpions, dragons and every device of Satan, and nothing shall by no means hurt or harm us. We know without a shadow of a doubt that God has our back, and he will not allow the devil to destroy us, but we still have our part to play. God will not give us victory without our effort, victory comes when we cry out to the Lord. God has an ear, and he hears every word that comes out of our mouth, that's why the word said: that the righteous cry out to the Lord and he hears and delivers them from all their troubles." (Psalm 34)

8. *Corporate Prayer*

The book of Acts is composed of several corporate prayers. We see the church coming together to pray over different situations.

When the people of God were multiplying rapidly, there were rumblings and discontent among Greek and Hebrew-speaking believers. The Greek-speaking believers because their widows were discriminated against in the daily food distribution. "So, the twelve disciples called a meeting with the believers and explained to them that they are called to teach and preach the Word, and not to distribute food, so they must select seven men who are well respected and who are full of the Spirit and wisdom and give them the responsibility. The seven men were presented before the Apostles, and they prayed and laid their hands on them." (Acts 6:1-6)

Even after Jesus had ascended into heaven, the disciples, along with Mary Magdalene, Mary the mother of Jesus, other women, and the brothers of Jesus, met together and were united in prayer." (Acts 1:14)

Corporate prayer is very effective in many ways: it brings the believers together, not just physically but in their hearts and minds, for one common goal and objective. There will be situations from time to time in which a person will not always have the strength to pray for themselves and will need other believers to pray with them in the situation. The scripture says, "One shall trace a thousand, but two shall put ten thousand to flight." This is saying that what one can do to experience victory, two can accomplish more and do more extraordinary things.

I believe with all my heart that if the believers cease acting independently of other believers and seek the help of others in prayer, it will resolve a lot of issues. Some persons undergo struggles as though they can overcome alone, not realizing or refusing to realize that they would have gotten a release if they pursued help. The Bible declares, iron sharpeneth iron. In other words, we learn from each other and grow. When we meet and pray, we will accomplish great things.

Let's examine what happened throughout the book of Acts when the Apostles and believers joined in prayers. Note: great things always happen when leaders lead from the front. The Apostles prayed together, recognizing the importance of leaders joining hearts, minds, spirits, and bodies as one. They destroyed the barrier of division, selfishness, pride, and competition and focused on the mission of God, not selfish desires. By doing so, they accomplished more for God than they would if they took an individualistic approach. They provided an example for us to understand the importance of working together to do the work of God.

We must remember that what we do is about God, pleasing him, and accomplishing the assignments He gives us daily. Unity is strength, but unfortunately, we as a church today miss it. Imagine today's leaders (Apostles, Prophets, Pastors, Teachers, Evangelists, etc.) laying aside their selfish conduct to join as one body (the body of Christ) in fellowship and prayer. In that case, we will see more people added to the body of Christ accompanied by miracles and more testimonies of victory.

Too many leaders are focused only on themselves and their ministries. Even among the local body of believers, you can scarcely find leaders working with each other because of the disunity. Always remember that when there is unity, there will always be a manifestation of the glory of God. If leaders refuse to work together and pray, how can we expect the regular believer to unite in prayer before God?

Peter was placed in prison directly after James was beheaded. He was placed between four squads of four soldiers and was bound with chains on his hands and feet. Herod was about to put Peter on public trial in the next twelve hours, but the church was United in prayer. The believers were determined to knock on heaven's door for Jehovah God to come to the rescue of his servant Peter. The church kept praying earnestly, in one accord, with one aim, with the same mindset, crying out to God until something happened. And guess what, the Lord sent an angel to deliver Peter out of the hands of Herod. (Acts 12)

I love how the Apostle describes the body of Christ. He used a literal body and made it clear that the hands can't say that he doesn't need the eyes, neither can he say he doesn't need the feet, and the ears can't say that he doesn't need anybody. (1 Corinthians 12). Paul emphasized with this parallel that as the body of Christ, we are not independent of each other, and we need each other to survive because if one person is affected, everyone should feel the effects. Jesus told his disciples to carry each other's burden and mourn with those who mourn. Unless we, the church, see the importance of corporate prayer, we will not see more results of God's manifestation.

8. Prayer of Decree and Declaration

A decree is a formal and authoritative order with the force of law, a judicial decree by royal decree—an official order issued by a legal authority. The prayer of decree involves speaking a prophetic word or words through the illuminating and impregnating power of the Holy Spirit. The word must be sound and can make what seems invisible visible. The prayer of decree basically commands things that are non-existent into existence from within the spiritual realm with immediate effect.

Here are a few examples:

- Ordering things we desire to be manifested and locate us wherever we are, in Jesus' mighty name.

- To order things to be developed and come to us.

- Use our mouths and speak words through the influence of the Holy Spirit to come forth, and when revealed, they possess a legal right to stay.

It is a royal decree. Only people from the royal family with a particular position can make such a decree because they have the King's permission, power, and authority. You will need to be at a place in God, in the realm of the Spirit, the supernatural, to be able to make such a decree. It takes believers who have a serious relationship with God and who know who they're in God to make a spiritual decree; Christ must be the Lord of their life.

A decree can only be issued by a legal authority. As believers (actively living by the Word of God and keeping His commands), we have the power to speak things into being and watch them manifest before our very eyes. This is because we are connected to the source (God) through which all things are created.

"Thou shalt also decree a thing, and it shall be established unto thee: and the light shall shine upon their ways." (Job 22:28)

When the believer decrees a thing (speak a prophetic word), it will manifest into something tangible. The word spoken does not go away but lingers into the atmosphere until it finds an avenue to work through. I know this may be like a large pill for some persons to take in, but you will eventually understand when we go into more detail.

Let's examine the word declare.

To declare is to say something solemnly and emphatically. To make known or state clearly, especially in explicit or formal terms. That is, to proclaim, announce, state, reveal, publicize, broadcast. A declaration is the result of a decree. A declaration is to make the decree known to the public. A declaration announces that what has been a decree has become a reality to the public. The correlation between decree and declare is that the declaration broadcasts the decree to ensure that the word spoken effectively produces a visible manifestation.

The story is told of a young man hoping to enter college, but neither he nor his family could afford the fees. Fortunately, he was a devoted child of God who believed and lived by the Word. One day he got up and decided to decree things over his life, "may the money for my school fees find me in full." Three days after the decree, he got a phone call from an uncle he hadn't heard from in years, saying he should stop by to collect five hundred thousand dollars. The money received was more than enough.
Overjoyed, he began to call friends and family to share the good news, even persons who weren't interested to hear. It is time to take back our rightful place in the Kingdom of God. Begin to speak things into existence in your life. Instead of

complaining daily and blaming others for your pain and disappointments, immerse yourself in God's Word and believe it.

Nothing will occur when our mouths remain sealed. Speak the word by faith over your life, children, family, and relatives. We must combat every negative thing over our lives with our decree in Jesus' Name. Let go of the past and focus on the present. Decree and declare what God desires for your life, and it shall come to pass.

The spoken word is powerful. Hebrews 4:12 declares, "the Word of God is quick and powerful, and sharper than any two-edged sword, piercing even to the dividing asunder of the soul and spirit, and of the joints and marrow, and is a discerner of the thoughts and of the heart."

The word of faith over your situation will bring an immediate result. When you speak the Word of God over your life or conditions, you must expect to see results. The prophet Jeremiah said, "when the Word came, I ate it up" (Jeremiah 15:16), and Ezekiel spoke that when the scroll was given to him, he ate it (Ezekiel 3:2). Both men indicated that when they received the Word of God, they fed on it; it was their food. The word went straight into their bodies and brought nourishment.

In the same way, God's word must become a part of us. Our output must reflect our input. The more we have the Word of God inside of us, the more we speak it with confidence. It is impossible to speak what is not within; therefore, if we are to be effective in prayer, we must know the Word of God so when difficulties arise, we will be able to speak it into our situations. In the book of Genesis, chapter one, it is expressed that after God created Heaven and the Earth, darkness was upon the face of the deep. And God said, let there be light, and there was light.

When God said let there be light, my interpretation is that something was opposing the light. But what did God do when he came under opposition? He used the Word (Logos). Nothing moved before God spoke; his presence did not change nor move anything, even though he is all-powerful and almighty. We know things shift when God speaks as the light appears at His command.

- What are some of the things that are opposing your life today?

- What is trying to stop our progress in life?

- What are some of the things Satan has put in your life to prevent you from being successful?

- What are some of the devices of hell for your life to create a block or hindrance?

- Who are the people creating stumbling blocks or hindrances to your progress?

Prayer of Declaration

Unless we start to decree and declare over our lives, things will not change. Things remain the same until we use God's Word to speak into every situation. Jesus said, "if you have faith and command that mountain to be removed and be cast into the sea it shall happen." All we need to do is speak the Word daily in our lives and circumstances and wait for the results. We must remember that we are in very serious warfare because we have an enemy who is trying everything to stop and destroy us. His name is Satan, and we must remain alert and sober to overcome his devices.

According to Psalm 2:8, whenever I ask God in prayer, He will give me the heathen for an inheritance and the uttermost part of the earth for my possession. I declare that the wealth of the wicked is stored up for the righteous in Jesus' name.

- Let all my enemies be put to shame and disgrace in the name of Jesus.

- Let everyone who has been opposing my life be removed by fire.

- Let the Holy Ghost and fire expose all my secret enemies.

- Let everyone who doesn't mean me well be exposed and put to shame.

- I declare that every pit the enemy digs for me, they will fall in it in Jesus' mighty name.

- I declare that the bow of the enemy is broken.

- I release fire against everything that has been opposing my life in Jesus' name.

- My God will surround me as He surrounds Jerusalem.

- I declare and decree by fire that no weapon formed against me, my children, career, and ministry shall prosper. Every tongue that rises against me in judgment is condemned (Isaiah 54:17)

- I declare that the blood of Jesus has already given me the victory.

- I am overcome by the blood and the words of my testimony.

- I was born to win and sentenced to succeed.

- I declare that they who are with me are more than they who are against me.

CHAPTER 7

The Power of Prayer

Prayer Disturbs, Immobilize, and Changes Demonic Atmosphere and Climates.

Here is a breakdown of the definitions:

- *Disturb* - to dislodge (move something from its place).

- *Immobilize* - to stop something from moving and working

- *Change* - to make someone or something different

- *Climate* - a region with prevailing weather conditions. It also signifies the prevailing trend of public opinion or another aspect of public life.

   a) Every climate and atmosphere have a different demonic operation.

b) There are different systems that have been established in different atmospheres.

Many Satanic headquarters operate in specific locations across the world.

- These locations are deemed special places and hold a building for the worshippers and followers of Satan, with the influence of the hierarchy of demons.

This is where Witches and Warlocks meet with worshippers as they glorify the devil and pray against the church. The Witches and Warlocks who lead these ceremonies are known to practice rituals that include the killing of human beings, preferably young people (because their blood is considered stronger, fresher, and richer). This is offered to the devil and then drank. The more blood they drink, the more power they receive, and the higher they go up in rank. Hence, blood is very important to the kingdom of Satan.

The followers of Satan who organize the death of those whose blood is desired by the witches and warlocks would grow closer to becoming a witch. Deaths instigated by witches for sacrifices usually unfold in different ways:

a) fatal crashes of vehicles, where blood is shed heavily

b) murders - shooting, stabbing, etc.

c) plane crashes

Success in these missions is an increase in rank for those involved in all these brutal activities. These are some important facts to note about these establishments and their operations.

- Satanic headquarters have been set up in every country. Some countries have more and larger headquarters because of their size.

- There are also other Luciferian meeting places other than the headquarters; some of them have disguised themselves. Many operate as churches and are using the name of Jesus to deceive the body of Christ.

- Many of the Pastors and leaders that you see today are not serving God but the devil, they are wolves in sheep's clothing, they are agents of the devil who are sent to destroy God's people.

They preach under the influence of demonic spirits; they also prophesy and do miracles under the influence of demons. Without the gift of discerning these spirits, one will not be able to recognize them. Don't be afraid of the things that you're reading about now because prayer will disturb, immobilize, and change these demonic atmospheres and climates. When we go to God in prayer, our prayers will render a lot of damage to the kingdom of darkness. Our prayers will go into satanic buildings and turn over satanic altars where sacrifices are offered to their demise.

Our Prayers are powerful and can stop the operations of witches, wizards, and warlocks, and bring them to naught in the Mighty Name of Jesus.

There is a penetration through opposing atmospheres when we pray; prayer will go in and through and stop satanic operations:

- *Concentration* - where Satan imposes his focus and powers upon individuals, a group of people, a church, or a territory to stop their purpose.

- *Satanic wombs* - satanic schemes that have manifested to bring pain, oppression, depression, sorrow, rejection, etc.

- *Spiritual abortions* - that which is dead before it manifests, by demonic spirits on assignment. Talents, dreams, and purpose.

- *Spiritual miscarriages* - the suppression and concentration of satanic schemes upon someone's life, to destroy their purpose and destiny.

In 1 Kings 18, the Prophet Elijah confronted Ahad, at a time when he and his evil wife Jezebel were doing all manner of evil in the sight of God. They had led the people into idol worship and had turned the Temple of God into their designated place to conduct their practices. Elijah boldly stood against their wickedness and rebellion. He exposed and brought to naught their worship of Baal and declared with evidence the supernatural power of God through prayer, professing that there was only one God in Israel, and He alone ought to be served. This happened when Elijah challenged Ahab to bring the 450 prophets of Baal, and the 450 prophets of Asherah who ate at the table of Jezebel to meet with him on Mount Carmel. Elijah said to the people, "how much longer will you waver, hobbling between two opinions? If God be God, follow him! But if Baal is God, follow him, but the people were completely silent." 1 Kings 18:21

The man of God sent for two bulls, and he gave one to the 950 prophets to cut into pieces then prepared an altar to call on their god, and he (Elijah) would cut his bull into pieces as well and prepare an altar. And Elijah said to the 950 prophets of Baal, call your gods and the god who answers by fire, he is the true God.

You know the story, the false prophets call on their gods from morning until noon and nothing happened, they even started cutting themselves which was to no avail. During this time Elijah was mocking them because their god would not answer. He repaired the altar and called on the Lord in prayer and the Lord heard him and sent fire on the altar and revealed who He was. Elijah then ordered that all the false prophets must be put to death.

Why did I bring up this example? Whenever a true man or woman of God prays, prayer will disturb, immobilize, and change the demonic atmosphere and climate. Always remember that our prayers can cause a lot of damage to the kingdom of Satan. We must pray in faith, not wavering but standing on the Word of God and He, God will back His Word.

Prayer Destroys Satanic Devices and Strategies
Definition of the terms:

a) *destroy* - to ruin or put an end to something

b) *device* - something that is made for a particular purpose.

c) *strategy* - a plan of action or policy designed to achieve a major or overall aim.

d) *plan* – a plan for military operations and movements during a war or battle.

e) *Science and art-* the science and art of employing the political, economic, psychological, and military forces of a nation or group of nations to afford the maximum support to adopt policies in peace or war.

When we look at the world today, we can see the techniques used by the Devil through the political systems, music, fashion, science, and technology to captivate the minds of people. These means are strategically used to invade and consume the Church of the living God.

In the political system, leaders all over the world have made laws that are contrary to the Word of God. Many have little or no fear for God, so they make decisions based according to their disposition or direction of the world rather than the direction of God. Even countries that have practiced Godly principles for years are slowly shifting from these practices and teachings. Countries like America and Jamaica, which were characterized by Godly structure, especially in their schools have removed Jesus to replace His teachings with other things. We must realize that this is a plan and strategy of the enemy, for the next generation to grow up without the knowledge and fear of God in them.

The world today is relying on science for answers to their questions and solutions to a life crisis, rather than looking to God. The truth is, we are living in a science-dominating time and people have believed in its capacity to provide the answers they need. The devil has skillfully resorted to using science as a weapon to pull people away from God and into confusion where they begin to doubt His very existence and power.

Let's look at Fashion and how the enemy uses it as a device. In recent years fashion has taken a turn. A lot of manufacturing companies are owned by satanic worshippers, and they are endorsing their belief through the signs and designs imprinted on their products.

What signs may you ask? I am talking about the Illuminati (an organization of Satan, which has its symbols and signs). The signs are seen all over the clothing in the form of the peace sign, pyramids, skulls, star of David, etc. In addition to the designs, male clothing has started to look more feminine because some fashion designers are homosexuals. When purchased and worn, other men are attracted to the customers, adding to their numbers.

Music is arguably the most powerful device the Devil uses to hold people in captivity when compared to the aforementioned. Music's influence and capacity to not only send messages through the lyrics but allure listening with the beat. The moment a beat is heard, it is easy to find your feet or hands moving, then your entire body. I believe that we were created with music in us, which allows us to easily express ourselves through music. The impact music has on people is undeniably mind-blowing.

Let's look at dancehall and hip hop and the effects on the young population. Dancehall music originated in Jamaica and is widely known around the world. Our young people have been influenced by this music in a very powerful way though the messages are usually gun-related, centered around girls, sex, and partying. Not only has dancehall provided entertainment, but many have been living the lyrics because it is considered a popular thing. As early as three years old, kids are seen singing dancehall songs but struggle to learn math, and phonics and speak fluent English. Music has become a huge weapon for the enemy, to get at the Kingdom of God. Although a lot of people enjoy gospel music, many are more interested in secular music.

The Bible said that we should not be ignorant of satan's devices, or he will take advantage of us (2 Corinthians 2:11). We can see where the devil is taking advantage of ignorant people who are not aware of the devices he has been using, to trap, bound and destroy lives and families.

We the people of God have a weapon called prayer, which can do damage to the strategies and devices of the enemy. Prayers can break curses placed on our lives through bad political decisions or music and destroy the jokes of the enemy over our children in the Mighty Name of Jesus.

We as the Church have the authority to bind the powers and systems of hell over our lives, country, and even the world at large, and to command them to be uprooted in the Name of Jesus. Release the presence of God over the device of hell so that God's presence will superimpose the devices of Satan.

It doesn't matter what the Devil plans he comes with, nothing will overthrow, overrule, condemn, or destroy the church of the living God. Why? Because the church was built on a solid foundation which is, the Rock, Jesus Christ Himself. He is overseeing His church and will not allow the enemy to destroy it.

Remember that Jesus is the Bride's Groom, and the Church is His Bride, He is married to the church, and loves His Bride dearly, so whatever or whoever desires to destroy the relationship will catch fire and burn. Every device or strategy that has been put in place will be destroyed in Jesus Mighty Name

"And I say unto thee, that thou art Peter, and upon this rock, I will build my church; and the gates of hell shall not prevail against it." Matthew 16:18 (KJV)

Believers have been given the power and authority to bind and to loose every power of darkness that has been fighting against the people of God, and everything that opposes the will of God on this earth and for our lives. In other words, we as God's chosen vessels, have the right to speak to every Satanic operation on this earth. Command them to cease or come to an end, and they will have to obey because Heaven agrees with us. Matthew 18:18 (KJV)

Webster's dictionary defines the word "bind" as "to make secure by tying; to confine, restrain, or restrict as if with a bond: to constrain with legal authority. It also means to arrest, apprehend, handcuff, lead captive, take charge of, lock up, restrain, check, or put a stop to. To loose means "to untie, to free from restraint, to detach, to disjoin, divorce, separate, unhitch, get loose, unbind, break away, get free, unchain, free, escape, release, liberate, unlock, disconnect and forgive.

There are so many things that People need to be loose from today:

- *Evil Spells* - a curse that has been placed over someone or something by a witch. Sometimes it is placed over a generation, family, or community.

- *Curse* - a solemn utterance intended to invoke a supernatural power to inflict harm or punishment on someone or something. This can also be a prayer or invocation for harm or injury to come upon one.

- *Demonization* - to portray (someone or something) as evil or worthy of contempt or blame, or to make into a demon, to bring under the control or influence of a demon.

- *Evil Inheritance* - something passed down from parents to their children. Inheritance is the right of ownership given to someone by law or through birthright to take over another person's estate. Inheritance can be in the form of cash, property, or position.

- *False teaching* - teachings that are contrary to the truth

- *Familiar spirit* - a demon supposedly attending and obeying a witch, often said to assume the form of an animal.

- *Ungodly vows (or inner vows)* - are declarations or promises we make to ourselves, which we set in our heart and mind to protect us from pain, using words like always and never.

- *Ungodly pledge* - a solemn promise or agreement to do or refrain from accepting God or a particular religious doctrine, or the practice of godly doings. It is sinful, wicked, and impious, not conforming to religious tenets or canons.

Ungodly soul ties - when two persons have become very attached; deeply bonded in their connection.

There are different ways in which you can be tied to someone:

- *Emotionally* - ties that are from similar experiences or emotions.

- *Spiritually* - a deep connection with someone spiritual, like a father to a son or a mother to a son/daughter.

- *Physically* - ties through sexual relationships or any sexual activity with someone.

There are other things that people need to be free from like sin, guilt, shame, depression, condemnation, manipulation, intimidation, mind control, religious control, sickness, disease, worldliness, etc.

With the authority of Almighty God, we can command all these things to loose their hold on people's lives in the Mighty Name of Jesus Christ of Nazareth, and they will have to obey.

We have been given the keys to unlock every cave or prison the Devil has placed people in or any conditions or circumstances that are holding people captive.

Prayer Releases and Fuels the Anointing
Definition of the terms:

- *Release* - allow or enable to escape from confinement; set free allow (something or someone) to move, act, or flow freely.

- *Fuel* - a substance such as coal, oil, or gasoline that is burned to provide heat or power, and it causes a fire to burn more intensely.

The Bible declares that when the day of Pentecost fully came, the Apostles and the others were all with one accord in one place. They could not be there looking out of space or talking, they were praying and praising God with the "spirit" of expectation and anticipation on the "promise" Jesus gave them, that they should stay in Jerusalem until they have been "clothed" with "Power" from a High. While they were there in one heart and spirit, the Bible said suddenly there came a sound from heaven as of a rushing, of a mighty wind, and it filled all the houses where they were sitting. And there appeared unto them cloven tongues of fire, and it sat upon each of them. And they were filled with the Holy Ghost, and began to speak with other tongues, as the Spirit gave them utterance. (Acts 2:1-4)

What is "Anointing"?

The anointing is the supernatural manifested presence of God. It is the outpouring and infilling presence of the Holy Spirit in the life of believers. This manifestation of the Holy spirit in and through the lives of believers illuminates, penetrates, and impregnates our being with fire. Different symbols in the Bible are used to describe the anointing:

- *Dew* - the Holy Spirit pours on us like tiny drops of water, falling on the believer's body causing it to get wet. (Daniel 4:15, 23,25) (Deuteronomy 33:13,28) (Genesis 27:28,39) (Hosea 6:4; 13:3; 14:5

- *Drizzle* - like light rain falling, the Holy Spirit falls on us lightly in preparation for the rain. (Isaiah 45:8)

- *Rain* - rain has a dual implication. First, as refreshing where there has been dryness and barrenness (Joel 2:23-29). Second, as restoration where there has been a loss (Isaiah 28:11-12)

- *Rivers* - a large natural stream of water flowing in a channel to the sea, a lake, or another such stream. John made it clear that the work of the Holy Spirit as of living water was to be available after the ascension of Jesus (John 7:37-39)

- *Wind* - the perceptible natural movement of the air, especially in the form of a current of air blowing from a particular direction. The Holy Spirit coming as wind depicts His power and guidance. The work of the Spirit breathes into lives, and something transpires that people cannot recognize. At Pentecost, the Holy Spirit came like a wind (Acts 2:3)

- *Dove* - the Holy Spirit, like a dove, is gentle, calm, and peaceful. At Jesus' baptism, the dove came and sat on Jesus. (Matthew 3:16)

- *Oil* - is directed to the Holy Spirit at work in our life; He makes us sensitive, holy, and full of wisdom (1 John 2:20)

- *Fire* - like fire, the Holy Spirit goes inside of us and burns everything that is not of God. He also burns our entire body with His presence. He purifies us from all evil and refines us as gold.

When the believers pray, their prayers go up to God as a sweet-smelling savor, and it will attract and draw the presence of God to us or among us.

Whenever God pours out His Spirit upon us, there will always be evidence of His manifestation. The anointing (which is the supernatural outpouring and indwelling presence of God) can do and will do wonders for us.

Evidence of the Anointing (the manifested presence of God):

The Anointing will lift burdens and destroy yokes
A burden is a load, typically a heavy one. It is a weight or source of pressure, borne by someone or something. A yoke is a wooden crosspiece that is fastened over the necks of two animals and attached to the plow or cart that they are to pull. Burdens and yokes are heavy and will restrict, restrain, and limit you.

The only difference between them is that the yoke is mainly placed around someone's neck (which brings limitations to vision, direction, and movements). While the burden can be on your back, shoulder, head, and on the inside of a person.

"And it shall come to pass on that day, that his burden shall be taken away from off thy shoulder, and his yoke from off thy neck, and the yoke shall be destroyed because of the anointing." Isaiah 10:27 (KJV)

There are so many people living today with burdens. They walk with it, sleep with it, work with it, and some even worship and pray to God with it. This world is filled with people struggling with various burdens because the Devil has inflicted them with his devices and schemes, to restrict and hinder the progress of God's people. Many have been oppressed by demonic activities, experiencing pressure or deep distress, mentally, psychologically, physically, and spiritually. Some are depressed because of the cares of this life, or unexpected circumstances that affect their minds, causing them to become weak, fragile, and vulnerable. Today, even believers are faced with depression.

During this time of crisis with Covid 19, many people around the world have been faced with uncertainties and are very discouraged as to what to do and where to go. Many are unsure of their job security in the aftermath of the virus. Thousands lost their jobs because companies were forced into permanent closure and many other disturbances unfolded, but prayer will release and fuel the anointing, lift every burden, and destroy every joke by fire.

The Anointing Will Break Down Prison Door
"And at midnight Paul and Silas prayed and sang praises unto God: and the prisoners heard them. And suddenly there was a great earthquake so that the foundations of the prison were shaken: and immediately all the doors were opened, and everyone's bands were loosed." Acts 16:25-26

Prison represents bondage. Unfortunately, this world is filled with people in bondages. There are so many kinds of bandages that people find themself in these days which can be frightening. Prison can be a system someone finds themselves attached to and could be a political, religious, cultic, or music system. Most of our government leaders are involved in a myriad of ungodly and evil systems today because of their greed for money and power.

It is so scary to see the things people are involved in to attain popularity or earn wealth. The painful part is that a lot of them want to come out or detach themself but lack the power to do so. Bad or hasty decisions have put a lot of people in a predicament today of suffering, crying out for help daily. I learned in life that money cannot make a person happy. If that were the case, many wealthy individuals would not be suffering from depression, and in extreme cases, they wouldn't have committed suicide. Others have turned to drugs for comfort and end up harming themselves.

I read an article a few years ago about the story of Cris Brown, a well-known male artist around the world. He made a statement that struck me which highlighted that when he goes on stage or moves around the world, people would see a superstar; a very popular and great artist from the outside, but on the inside, he was a little boy crying for help. We see a lot of people daily, movie stars, sports stars, great entertainers, etc. who look okay from the outside but are in prison and need freedom. Everyone has their own prison situation but is crying on the inside for help even though it's not obvious.

Let me assure you today that prison doors can be torn and ripped into pieces by praying aggressively against every prison condition and commanding the door to be open and the chains to fall off God's people in the Mighty Name of Jesus.

Prayer Move the Hand of God
Do you know that God has hands? and that He can stretch them forth to help us and destroy our enemies.

"Behold, the Lord's hand is not shortened, that it cannot save; neither his ear heavy, that he cannot hear." Isaiah 59:1 (KJV)

Intense and persistent prayer can cause God to release His hands and do wonders for us. God has ears and will give heed to our prayers. He will not neglect the cry of His people. The Bible declares that when the righteous cry for help, the Lord hears and delivers them out of all their distress and troubles. Psalm 34:17 (AMP)

There is a certain cry, that whenever it reaches God, it will pull His hands to work on our behalf. This is the kind of cry the Children of Israel made when they were in Egypt and were being mistreated by the slave masters.

"And the Lord said, I have surely seen the affliction of my people which are in Egypt, and have heard their cry by reason of their slave master; for I know their sorrows, and I am come down to deliver them out of the hand of the Egyptians, and to bring them up out of that land unto a good land flowing with milk and honey; unto the place of the Canaanites, and the Hittites, and the Amorites, and the Perizzites, and the Hivites, and the Jebusites." Exodus 3:7-8 (KJV)

Prayer will move the hand of God to:

Fight our battles
As children of God, we face many battles each day. The situations we encounter in life daily are sometimes serious and bring fear to our hearts. At times we feel as if we are between a rock and a hard place, with nowhere to turn, neither to the left, right, front nor back. It's as if the enemy traps us in a place where he can manipulate us.

In 2 Chronicles 20, three nations, Ammon, Moab, and Mount Seir came up against the People of God to destroy them. Then, Mount Seir's army alone was big enough to overcome the army of Judah, Hence, the alliance with the other two armies naturally would indicate a sure defeat of the people. King Jehoshaphat saw that Judah was in trouble because they were not able to challenge the three nations or even win. The bible stated that the King was terrified and in distress, but God sent His prophet to comfort his heart and advise him not to be fearful. He was also reminded that the battle is not his but the Lord's. The Prophet of God went on further to tell the King to get the army ready to go down to meet their enemies the following day, and that they will not need to fight the battle; but only to take up their position, stand still, and see the deliverance of the Lord who is with them.

After King Jehoshaphat received the Word of God from the Prophet, he consulted the people, then he appointed singers to sing to the Lord and praise him in the beauty of holiness, as they went out. And when they began to sing and praise, the Lord caused the armies of Ammon, Moab, and Mount Seir to start fighting against each other killing all the army men. (2 Chronicles 20)

Have you ever been faced with a battle you believed you could not overcome? Just begin to pray and believe God, then you will see His divine intervention. God will not disappoint His people, and He will always be on time to deliver us from the hands of the enemy.

To Bring Protection
Protection is keeping someone safe from harm or injury. It is to cover or shield from exposure, injury, damage, or destruction. Believe it or not, we are in a world that is full of evil. It is so easy for people to give in, and practice evil rather than good. The Devil has mastered his crafts and has used them to perfection to trick and persuade people to give into demonic practices, where they will practice all sorts of iniquity. Everywhere you go, you will find people who have dedicated themselves to the practices of evil. You don't know who to trust these days because even your very own family members have been drawn into a corrupt lifestyle. Without the eyes of the Spirit, you will not know the wicked intentions of those around us or who we encounter.

Some people today will go the extra mile to hurt innocent persons, even spending their last money with the obeah man to work witchcraft on while forsaking their needs for bills, food, clothes, and other personal items. People will go into the cemetery and communicate with the dead to do ill. Others will have sex with animals to release a curse on people.

Parchment paper is also used for the practice of witchcraft. A person with an ill-intent would write another's name and bury it or put it in bottles and throw it into the sea. Others would go to the sea and communicate with the queen of the course, and pay the demon to inflict sickness, disease, and demons, and cause a lot of bad to happen. It doesn't matter the evil which has come up against you, or the evil people are doing to you, even the things sent after you and your family, cannot affect or infect you because prayer will move the hands of God to bring protection over you and your family.

Psalm 91:1-8 declares, "He that dwelleth in the secret place of the most High shall abide under the shadow of the Almighty. I will say of the Lord, He is my refuge and my fortress: my God; in him will I trust. Surely, he shall deliver thee from the snare of the fowler, and from the noisome pestilence. He shall cover thee with his feathers, and under his wings shalt thou trust: his truth shall be thy shield and buckler. Thou are not afraid of the terror by night; nor the arrow that flieth by day. Nor for the pestilence that walketh in darkness; nor the destruction that wasteth at noon. A thousand shall fall at thy side and, and ten thousand at thy right hand; but it shall not come nigh thee. Only with thine eyes shalt thou behold and see the reward of the wicked."
We don't need to be afraid of the evil that is in the world. Our responsibility is to be persisting in prayer and believe in the power of God to protect us from evil doers and the assignments of the devil.

Always remember that evil cannot overcome good, and darkness cannot overcome the light, neither can the system or devices of Satan can destroy or stand in the way of God or contain the power of the Holy Spirit. The Devil is terrified by the very mention of the name of Jesus.

Prayers Against Demonic interference and attacks

- May my prayers have clear access to the throne of Heaven, and may they not be earthbound.

- May the God that answers by fire answer me by fire, in the Mighty Name of Jesus Christ.

- May the God of the Now answer me speedily.

- May the God of the Sudden answer me quickly.

- I stand in the Power of the Holy Ghost in the Name of Jesus Christ.

- I stand on the prophetic Word of God that declares, "I have given you the keys, and whatsoever you bind on earth, shall be bound in Heaven, and whatsoever you loose on earth shall be loose in Heaven."

- I bind every legal or illegal covenant I have made with the enemy, knowingly and unknowingly in the Mighty Name of Jesus.

- I release myself from the holds of the enemy.

- I cut all ties with the enemy knowingly and unknowingly in Jesus' Name.

- I bind the works and assignments of witches and warlocks in Jesus' Mighty Name. May their powers be broken and may their systems and assignments backfire in the Mighty Name of Jesus.

- May all their altars catch fire and burn to ashes in Jesus' Mighty Name.

- May their meeting places catch fire now in Jesus' Name.

- Holy Ghost Fire! Be released against every work of evil that witches and warlocks perform in Jesus' Mighty Name.

- May every spell that witches have sent for my life and my family catch fire now, in Jesus' Name I pray.

- I release myself from every inherited bondage in Jesus' Mighty Name.

- I release myself from every spiritual attachment in Jesus' Name.

- I release myself from every agreement with poverty in the Name of Jesus.

- I loose myself from lack, in the Mighty Name of Jesus.

- I break and loose myself from every inherited covenant in the mighty Name of Jesus Christ.

- I break and loose myself from every evil spell in the Mighty Name of Jesus.

- I break and loose myself from every evil curse in Jesus' Name.

- I release myself from every demonic stronghold in the mighty name of Jesus Christ.

- I break and release myself from every soul tie in Jesus' Mighty Name.

- I cut myself loose from the attachment of sickness generated through my family line, in the mighty name of Jesus Christ.

- I cut myself loose from every ungodly vow I have made with the enemy, knowingly or unknowingly, in the powerful name of Jesus Christ.

- Every evil substance or food that I have consumed, may I vomit them up now, in the mighty name of Jesus Christ of Nazareth.

- I command my body to resist every poisonous substance in Jesus' Name.

Amen.

About the Author

Kirton Whyte

Kirton O. Whyte has been a minister of the gospel for over 15 years. He is a father, husband, and spiritual mentor. Whyte has a bachelor's degree in Bible and Theology/Counselling and has been anointed and appointed by God as a Prophet, Evangelist, Counsellor, Preacher, and Teacher of the Word.

His mission is to reach as many people as possible with the gospel of Jesus Christ. God's impregnating and illuminating word has the power to bring men to repentance. When people accept the gospel, they need to be correctly discipled, and his founding ministry facilitates this.

He is the founder of Prophetic Hour, aired on his social media platforms, which has been touching and changing thousands of lives worldwide.

Hold Your Breath is an inspiring book that will benefit many who believe that nothing good will come out of their lives. Furthermore, it will be a propelling instrument that will resurrect visions and dormant ideas and bring readers comfort, hope, and joy.

This book depicts a life of defeat, bandage, and misery to a victorious life through Jesus due to submission to His perfect will.

Author's Contact Information:

Name: Prophet Kirton Whyte

Email: prophetwhyte7@gmail.com

Facebook: Prophet Kirton Whyte

Instagram: kirtonwhyte

www.ingramcontent.com/pod-product-compliance
Lightning Source LLC
Chambersburg PA
CBHW072135160426
43197CB00012B/2121